Letters
to a Young Madman

A MEMOIR

PAUL GRUCHOW

This book was designed by Connie Kuhnz.
Composition by BookMobile Design and Digital Publisher Services,
Minneapolis, Minnesota.

Levins Publishing
2300 Kennedy Street Northeast
Suite 160
MINNEAPOLIS MN 55413
612-238-0989
www.LevinsPublishing.com

Distributed by Itasca Books
www.itascabooks.com

ISBN 978-0-9853972-3-4
LCCN 2012938184

Printed in the United States of America

You desire to know the art of living, my friend? It is contained in one phrase: make use of suffering.

HENRI FREDERIC AMIEL

Foreword

Paul Gruchow began work on *Letters to a Young Madman* in June, 2003.

Earlier that spring, I had sent him several poems of mine which explored the life and work of Vincent van Gogh. Paul liked and critiqued them—then sent back two pages of prose. His subject was not the natural world, about which he'd written extensively, but mental illness and his experience of being a patient within the mental health treatment system. He was reaching deeply into himself and widely into the vast literature of human suffering.

When early drafts of *Letters* seemed disjointed, Paul wondered how journal entries, poems, stories, prayers, brief quotes and medical research could all cohere in the same book. I suggested he read Eduardo Galeano, whose elliptical style became a useful model.

As the writing evolved through summer and fall, I recall a conversation in which Paul lamented that his previous work was "of no importance" as literature or as an instrument of social change. He wanted to write transparently about childhood trauma, about the stigma of psychiatric diagnosis, and about how the treatment system infantilizes patients. Having been blocked for several years, he was, happily, at work again.

There were times when he almost convinced me, and other friends, that *Letters* would save him. A Christmas visit to the small house he'd purchased in Duluth, Minnesota, was encouraging. There was a sense of order and harmony. Paul was cooking again—one of his favorite avocations—and a version of the manuscript he'd been working on for six months was sitting on the living room table. He spoke passionately about giving voice to the mentally ill and the homeless, as he once had spoken about empowering environmentalists and rural people. When we watched a movie together—*What About Bob?*—in which a neurotic patient drives his narcissistic psychotherapist mad, Paul rolled on the floor, laughing in cathartic delight.

By mid January, 2004, insomnia, migraine headaches, debilitating depression and anxiety returned. This man who, like Thoreau, derived such joy from walking everywhere, could no longer summon enough energy to walk outside. As Jon Anderson wrote in his elegy for a mentally ill 19th century English poet, "John Clare's madness nature could not straighten."

During his adult life, Paul made several attempts at suicide. On February 22, 2004, at age 56, he died of a self-induced prescription drug overdose. Although he had found again his brilliant literary voice, he fought for but did not regain his mental health. *Letters,* his final work, is the important testimony of a brave and generous man.

I would like to thank the following individuals for their generous assistance in reading and offering suggestions that were helpful in preparing *Letters to a Young Madman* for publication: Dr. Diane Forsyth, Teresa Dutko, Sara Underhill, Calista Bockenstette, and Mark Schroeder.

Louis Martinelli
February 22, 2012

Letters
to a **Young Madman**

Against Amusement

The primary difficulty in writing a book such as this is that it cannot meet the test of what is vulgarly known as a good read: it cannot be amusing. Or perhaps more precisely, it cannot be both amusing and truthful. It can be *funny*; laughter and tears are constant companions; the difference between situational comedy and life is that while both provoke laughter, situational comedy never breaks your heart. A writer who wants to be perfectly amusing should imagine a place where nobody is an alcoholic, no one has aimed high and utterly failed, no husband beats his wife, no priest has ever had a hankering for little boys, no fourteen-year-old boy still wets the bed, no sixteen-year-old girl makes herself throw up in the toilet after every meal, no chain store ever cuts prices until the local merchant is driven into bankruptcy, no Norwegian bachelor hears terrible voices urging him to kill his mother in the name of God, no storm cloud ever carries the hail that destroys the crops, no youth has ever been sent to war—a place "where every man is good looking, every woman is strong, and every child is above average." There, you could be amused forever and ever, and you need never know the heights and depths to which human beings are ordinarily called. But what purpose might this serve? Is life so awful that we can't be serious about it for a minute? Is nothing worth a quarter of an hour's sobriety?

Heroes 1

Therapists have written a great many volumes of case studies invariably purporting to demonstrate the triumphs of sufferers over their psychological distresses, but if one reads them carefully, one cannot help seeing that the hero, in the end, is always the omniscient and all-wise therapist. I don't think there is another literature quite so saturated with self-appreciation as that created by psychotherapists. Of course, it could not be otherwise. As the African proverb says, "Until lions have their own historians, histories of the hunt will glorify the hunter."

Survival 1

Psychological patients are as wont to write stories of triumph over madness as are their psychologists. This is, after all, the classic, three-part story: man or woman fulfills early promise, is struck down by adversity, and finds redemption, usually in love. There used to be another kind of story, the tragedy, in which someone rises to great heights and then is destroyed by an equally great flaw of character. We don't much tell tragedies anymore. They are not, I suppose, suitable to our optimistic times.

This is the true story of the madman: a person fails to rise, has nowhere to fall from, muddles along, and eventually dies. Samuel Beckett wrote madman stories, but they have never made a literary genre. At least for people who suffer from severe depression, there is supposed to be no need for such stories. After all, it is said, eighty percent of those who suffer from depression can be successfully treated with modern medications and other therapies. I doubt this statistic. For one thing, the same success rate was claimed for treatment induced by nausea, by water torture, by insulin shock, by dozens of other barbarities of the past. It is an interesting phenomenon that, while many treatments have been proposed for the mentally ill, and later abandoned, all of them have been said, at one time or another, to have the same remarkably high success rate. For another thing, I know many people who are mentally ill. This is the story of most of them: they take their meds, they see their doctors, they go to the hospital from time to time, and they continue to struggle and suffer. The name of the story is not triumph or redemption, but survival.

My own story does not end with me bathed in bright sunlight and the Hallelujah Chorus playing in the background. It ends with me alive, more so some days than others. That has to be enough, because it's all there is.

Heroes 2

Once, in my dissolute youth, I went on a psychedelic trip. The first three or four hours of it were zany fun. This was in the days when television stations, like saloons, shut up shop at one a.m. After a brief religious exhortation and a rendition of the national anthem, the television screen went momentarily blank, and then test patterns played all through the night. A friend and I, flying high, watched these test patterns with infantile intensity and delight. They were the funniest things we had ever seen. We howled. We cried. We stomped our feet. We punched each other in glee. We rolled and writhed on the floor, our arms wrapped around our chests to contain the mirth. We screamed, we pointed, we giggled, we roared. We beat our fists into the carpet. Never had two young men been more hugely entertained. We probably would have been equally amused by a pair of rattles or rubber duckies, but those test patterns, they were groovy, man, they were far out.

As dawn was breaking, and the television stations were signing on again, the amusement abruptly ceased. The words emanating from the television set began to speak of a massive force of undercover agents that had been dispatched to hunt us down. There was an eerie stirring in the curtains. In the hallway outside my apartment door, the floorboards creaked ominously. A loud burst of noise from upstairs might have been made by a flushing toilet or it might have been the sound of shattering glass as someone forcibly entered the building. I cowered in a dark corner of the living room, behind the couch and away from the windows, trembling.

Eventually, I had to go out for a package of cigarettes. The store was just across the street from my apartment building, but it was a terrible ordeal to get there and back. I had, first, to summon the courage to open the apartment door. One never knew who might be lurking just outside it. With as much stealth as possible, I eased open the lock and determined, with many quick peeks, that it might be safe to go into the hall. As soon as I had, footsteps sounded on the stairway. My heart pounded. I darted back into my apartment and listened at the door until I was pretty sure the menace had passed. I gritted my teeth, clenched my fists, and forced myself to go out into the hallway again. After a long surveillance at the window in the front door of the apartment building, I got the courage to step onto the sidewalk.

I had been hiding in the dark behind drawn curtains. The morning sun shone with the searing light of a torture chamber. I could not begin to be certain that there were not ultra-high-intensity lights hidden in the architecture of the street and in the gratings of the sidewalk to highlight my movements. Agents undoubtedly crouched on rooftops behind chimneys, watching my every move through specially designed periscopes. The trees in the boulevard leaned towards the sidewalk at such an angle as to suggest that they had been rigged to fall upon me when I passed them. I had to walk in the grass at the edge of the street curb to foil this sinister plan. I walked as someone does who is being watched.

When I got to the edge of the street I had to cross, I paused. I leaned up against a lamppost, and closed my eyes to summon the composure to continue. The street was heavy with morning traffic. The engines of the cars had been outfitted with high frequency sirens that screamed in my ears. Several of them seemed to lurch in my direction as they passed the intersection. I had no doubt that their drivers were aiming for me and had been called off at the last minute by the agents on the rooftops, who preferred that I be killed in the street itself, to make it look like an accident. I waited a long time until there was a large enough gap in the traffic to attempt a crossing. Just as I put my foot onto the pavement, a car on the avenue pulled out onto the main street. I leaped back onto the boulevard. I would have run to hide, but there was no safe place to go. The forces against me were everywhere. At last another gap appeared in the traffic. I bolted across the street, pausing on the far corner to catch my breath and to try to calm my nerves.

I realized with despair that although I was not so far from my apartment—only across the street—that I was beyond salvation. The thing to do was to get those cigarettes and return to my apartment as quickly as possible, but not so quickly as to attract attention to myself. Even though there was somebody just inside the door who might have been an agent, I willed myself into the store. The grocery shelves were like the trees. They leaned precariously into the aisles. It was hard to imagine how the stock stayed put on them. The thought had crossed my mind that I might get something for breakfast, too, but that was out of the question. I was not so dumb as to head down one of those aisles.

I went to the cashier and asked for a box of Marlboros. The woman wanted to see identification. I knew that the game was up. The Musak was telling me so. To other people it might just have sounded like lousy music, but I could hear the low voices in the background chanting, "We've got you now, Paul, we've got you now, Paul." I pulled out my wallet and showed my driver's license. The cashier studied it. She was probably stalling while she found the trigger to the alarm with her foot. And then a police officer slipped into line behind me. I began to sweat and to quiver. I had to open my mouth in order to breathe. There was nowhere to run. I had to try to stay cool. After what seemed like ten minutes, the cashier returned my driver's license, handed me the Marlboros and rang up the sale.

"Keep the change," I said. I walked toward the door with studied poise, looking back only once to see if the cop was following me. When I was out the door, and although I knew it to be a mistake, I made a desperate, all-out sprint for my apartment, ignoring the curses of the driver who had screeched to a halt to avoid hitting me, not stopping to pick up the purse I knocked out of a woman's hand. Once I was inside my apartment, I locked and bolted the door and jammed a chair up under the doorknob. I went around and locked all the windows, pulled the shades, drew the curtains, I unplugged the television set and disconnected the telephone so that they could not be used to spy on me. And then I went into my bedroom, closed, locked, and barricaded the door, and climbed into bed. I pulled the covers over my head and lay, couched in the fetal position, like a small child, clutching a pillow for security. I prayed, out loud, that God might let this cup pass from me.

In about twenty-four hours I came down. My eyes felt like they were being propped open with saucers. It would be several days before I recovered from the exhaustion, but I was all right. I resolved that that would be my last encounter with hallucinogens, and it was.

But here's the thing. I know a man who needs an hour to climb a story of stairs and the better part of an afternoon to walk a city block because every time he crosses over a threshold or steps over a crack he first has to subdue the raging demons that are on the other side of it. I know a woman who, a long time ago, got a bad haircut and who has been in suicidal despair ever since. She cannot pass a mirror or shop window without looking into it to study her hair. She sees big bald spots where her hair has been gashed out. She sees that the hair on one side of her face is several inches long and on the other side is only an inch long. She sees bangs that are wildly uneven. She sees a frazzle of split ends. And she sees an incredibly ugly woman. None of these things, of course, is true to any observer, but they are true to her, and she struggles to talk or think of anything else. I know a man of astounding intelligence who would like to be a writer and has worked at becoming one for more than thirty years, but who has been defeated in every attempt because his mind races so uncontrollably that he cannot get to the end of even one sentence.

None of these people can go to bed for a few hours, get up quite recovered, and say, "I guess I'll never do that again." Except in the advent of miraculous new cures, these friends of mine are condemned to get up every morning of their lives and repeat the same nightmares all over again. Despite that, not one of them is bitter or defeated. They all have bright senses of humor, lively and engaging personalities, and enough fortitude and determination to shame generals. It takes as much courage for any one of them to persevere from one day to the next as has ever been required of any soldier with a chest full of medals. To me, they are heroes.

Heroes 3

We support these heroes—you and I do through our governments—at the rate of barest survival. We condemn them to lifetimes of dingy sleeping rooms, furnished out of dumpsters, in rattletrap buildings and dangerous neighborhoods, of soup kitchen meals, of clothes scrounged for free, of ill-fitting second hand shoes, of life disconnected in every material way from modern society. We are willing to buy their medicines at rates that give the drug companies generous profits. We are willing to pay their doctors handsome salaries. We are willing to subsidize their affluent landlords. But the afflicted themselves we expect to live in squalid poverty and to go to their graves innocent of any such thing as an amenity.

Self-esteem, Self-disgust

I know a man who, when he is sober, is paralyzed by doubt and depression, but who, when he is drunk, thinks himself one of the most interesting and talented human beings on earth. These beliefs are not, it seems to me, contradictory. They both emerge out of the struggle between what one hopes for and what one is capable of achieving. This struggle is common to the human condition. Rare and blessed is the person who is content to be what he or she was called to be.

. . . the solipsism of blank days . . .

ADAM HASLETT

Therapy 1

One day, early in my Dialectical Behavior Therapy (DBT), I started to talk about the events in my life that, I believe, precipitated my plunge into depression. My therapist quickly cut me off. "That's history," he said, "We're going to concentrate on the here-and-now." I didn't try to raise the subject again. There are, certainly, strong arguments to be made for the here-and-now approach to therapy:

1) It is one thing to come to terms with the past. Wallowing in it is quite another matter. And people like me, pessimists by nature, are expert wallowers. We take perverse delight in rehearsing our failures, nursing slights, rebukes, and rejections, and magnifying the powers of our enemies. We feed the flames of our current miseries with the fuel of our accumulated disappointments. It is undoubtedly helpful for someone to step in and say, "Enough already! Let's get on with life."

2) Every life is punctuated by setbacks, losses, injustices. In some people these blows provoke withdrawal and depression. In others, they strengthen resolve, and bestow renewed sense of purpose. I once worked with a man whose ego outstretched the boundaries of the universe. He was, in consequence, almost impossible to work with. Our literary agent confessed to me one day that after our project was completed, he intended never to have anything to do with the man again. And, indeed, the day our project was done, he telephoned the man and told him as much. Within minutes, my phone rang. My partner was on the line, breathless with excitement. "I have some tremendous news," he exclaimed. "We have finally gotten rid of that crummy agent!" I envied the man that day, and, in a limited sense, I still admire him. His confidence in himself was such that he simply could not be defeated. Those of

us who are prone to depression don't need megalomania, but we certainly do need, as an early priority, better skills at protecting ourselves from defeat. There will always be time later for post-mortems.

3) One of the delusions that people like me are vulnerable to is the belief that the past is destiny. A member of a social center for the mentally ill where I once worked approached me one day to report that she was being threatened by another member. She wanted me to ask him to leave. "Could you tell me what he is doing to threaten you?" I asked.

"Well, he's not doing anything right now, but he's going to," she said.

"We used to live at the same group home," she said, "and he said something there that made me cry."

I'll tell you what," I said. "I'll keep an eye on him, and if he does anything to threaten you, let me know right away. Okay?" This satisfied her.

It was a troubling and enlightening moment for me, because I recognized my own vulnerabilities in hers. I, too, if in less obvious ways, expected to be hurt, even by people of good will, and this is often a self-fulfilling expectation. One of the reasons I quit writing for several years was that I had convinced myself that no matter what I said, it would be ignored. I believe that this is a characteristic pattern of thought in people prone to depression. The only way out of this delusion, and out of the depression that follows from it, is to step from the past into the present.

There is, however, one very serious drawback to the here-and-now school of psychotherapy. To express no interest in the history of an emotional crisis is to assume that every emotional crisis is, at least for therapeutic purposes, pathological. But most depression, to take one example, is perfectly normal. A spouse or good friend dies. You lose your job. Your marriage ends in divorce. One of your children is arrested. The book you labored over for years is published and then remaindered without public notice. You contract a potentially fatal disease. If you *don't* feel depressed for a time, there is something wrong with you. When a normal emotion is pathologized, as often happens in psychotherapy, the patient is taught a very new way to be defeated. Now you are no longer merely depressed. You are *sick*.

Placebos

Blue placebos work better than red ones, except among Italian men. Injected placebos are more effective than pills. Brand-name placebos outperform generics. People who take their placebos regularly get more benefit than those who take them intermittently. Germans respond better than people from other nations to placebos for ulcers but less well to placebos for hypertension. In controlled studies, patients whose doctors think they might be getting a real medication respond better than patients of doctors who know the pills are placebos. When a new medication is introduced, the effectiveness of the medication it replaces falls dramatically.

Silence

The effects of silence accumulate. The silence of one person alone magnifies prayer, meditation, thought, the music of the universe. The silence of two friends is a communion; silence between two enemies cultivates fear and loathing. Silence in a crowd breeds solidarity, anxiety, embarrassment, or laughter, depending upon the circumstances. But the silence of millions is the cornerstone of evil.

The poem I dream has no flaws until I try to realize it.

FERNANDO PESSOA

What someone is begins to be revealed when his talent abates, when he stops showing what he can do.

FRIEDRICH NIETZSCHE

Clinical Depression 1

People who have had a brush with the blues think they know something about what it is like to be clinically depressed, but they don't. Clinical depression is as much like the ordinary blues as a wart is like cancer. It is a state of being suspended halfway between ordinary vitality and a coma. It is an illness in which your sensory systems shut down. Food becomes tasteless, any kind of sound oppressive. Colors fade to shades of nondescript gray. The light in the morning is only a slight variation on the light at midnight. Your chest constantly feels as if someone were standing on it. It seems like a lump in your throat, only the lump is strangling your heart. You want to cry but can't. You crave sleep, but it won't come. You lie in bed all day anyway because sitting up would take more energy than you possess. You feel as though you have come down with some devastating tropical fever. You hope desperately to die. You don't want to die to end the misery. You want to die because you are quite certain that the world would be better off without you, that it, in fact, wishes you to be dead. You would gladly do the deed yourself if you only had the strength.

Clinical depression is paranoid. Your closest friends, it seems, no longer care about you. Your boss secretly wishes you to fail. The publisher to whom you sent a manuscript two weeks ago is not considering it; on the contrary, she has just called a meeting of her staff to mock it. Sometimes clinical depression is grandiose: If I were to die, people would at last realize the prize they are missing. Sometimes it is self-pitying: I've botched everything; I wasn't even a good baby. Often it is self-destructive: I have quit several jobs I cherished for no other reason than I was depressed.

In a state of clinical depression absolutely nothing is funny. And such depression abhors tenderness. To have somebody fussing over you is as annoying as it would be to be engulfed by a swarm of horseflies. You just want everybody to go away and leave you alone. When they do, you despair over their neglect of you. Clinical depression is not, as one might think, a time of deep emotion; it is, rather, caught up in a single, vague, all-consuming emotion that is like a shallow version of regret. You regret everything, but not enough to do anything about it. Every exertion requires extraordinary effort, as if you were trying to function at the bottom of an ocean. You are condemned in a clinical depression to think about nothing but yourself, and you loathe, find ugly, besotted, putrid, absolutely everything about yourself. To be in a clinical depression is to experience a third dimension in which you are still technically alive but incapable of living.

I once sat at my desk for three straight days, intent upon stamping an envelope. For the three previous months, I had sat at the same desk trying, without success, to write the next sentence in the essay I was working on. I had given up on the essay and was now willing to settle for mailing a letter. From waking until bedtime, I sat there, staring first at the stamp, and then at the envelope. I scolded myself, I begged myself, I prayed to God that I might find the willpower to lift my hand from the desk, pick up the stamp, and put it on the envelope. I tried to shame myself. This is the only thing I'm asking of you, I said. When you have put the stamp on the envelope, you can sleep for twenty years, you can kill yourself, you can sit here at this desk until the flesh falls from your bones, but first, you have to put the stamp on the envelope. Is that too much to ask? But I could not do it. My muscles would not move. It was as if I were quadriplegic. At the end of the third day, I still had not stamped the envelope, but I finally managed to call my doctor. That is what clinical depression is like.

When I reached my doctor, I had difficulty making myself heard. In my humiliation my arm shook so violently that I couldn't hold the receiver to my mouth. I've finally got to admit it, I was thinking. I'm a lunatic. I'm a nutso. I'm a case for the funny farm. Any minute now I'll start to drool. I could see myself being hauled away in a straightjacket. This is what the stigma of clinical depression is like.

Clinical Depression 2

Here is one quick way to tell clinical depression from the blues. Ask yourself why you are depressed. If you can answer the question, you do not have clinical depression.

Clinical Depression 3

It is recess time at my country school. I am seven. The other twelve children are playing on the playground. I am on the opposite side of the building, huddled against the wall. I am crying. I have not been hit. I have not been insulted. I have not been excluded from the game. I am not ill. I adore the teacher. Nothing is the matter with me. I just can't stop crying.

Once when I came over to visit, in the woes of a depression born of love gone bad, my grandmother shook her finger at me and said, "I am psychiateest. You weel be arteest some day. Right now I geeve you wine."

LOUIS MARTINELLI

Clinical Depression 4

Depression is like a military action. It destroys in order to save.

I regard depression as the consequence of attempts to stifle life.

ALICE MILLER

Defense

Depression's purpose is defense.

I once met two wildly exuberant young men on a trail in Glacier National Park. At first I thought that they were stoned. But then their tale spilled out. They had come around a bend in the trail, they said, only to discover that they were sharing it with a grizzly bear. The bear was two or three hundred yards ahead of them. It sniffed, grunted, stood on its hind legs. The young men knew that trouble was coming. They did what you are instructed to do. They dropped slowly to their knees, and bent down, as if in genuflection. They brought their arms forward to cover their heads. They waited. The bear roared and charged. It stopped so short of them that they could see the hairs on its legs and smell its breath. But it did not attack. Perhaps forty-five minutes later another hiker came along and found them still huddled in their defensive posture. He had watched the encounter through binoculars from across the valley. "You can get up now. The bear's gone," he said.

Depression is just such a defensive posture. When the self feels threatened by an overwhelming force, it goes into hiding, and the body curls inward upon itself and sleeps. Only a long time after the danger has passed do body and self draw up the courage to expose themselves to the world again.

Loss 1

The subject of depression is loss.

One might lose a great many things: innocence, affection, friendship, employment, face, public esteem, possessions, independence, health, faith, prestige, honor, direction, purpose, hope, courage, humor, self-control, opportunity, love, freedom, permission, selfhood, and ultimately, life.

But what is merely lost can be found again. And what cannot be recovered can be done without. And what cannot be done without, one never truly had. Epictetus said that happiness lies in knowing that everything came from somewhere else and may at any moment return to the place from which it came.

Depression arises out of an unwillingness to relinquish what one never had, or out of an inability to make do with what one has, or out of the failure to search for what is lost. It does not see that loss is not a thing, but a state of mind. Things are what they are, but the mind can be changed.

Loss 2

Loss thrives in the medium of ingratitude. Instead of giving thanks for what has been, we regret what is to come. But we cannot know what is to come. So the sense of loss is rooted in the fear of the unknown. And the way out of loss leads us into the present.

Suffering

What does not destroy me makes me stronger.

This is Friedrich Nietzsche's best-known remark. It reminds me of something John Berryman said not long before he killed himself: "I hope almost to be crucified." Both men led celebrated and tortured lives. Both sought meaning in pain, as those who have suffered greatly must. Both were notably witty. "Perhaps I know why it is man alone who laughs," Nietzsche said. "He alone suffers so deeply that he had to invent laughter." And on another occasion, "[W]e should call every truth false which was not accompanied by at least one laugh." "Sleeping is no mean art: for its sake one must stay awake all day," he said. And, "A pair of strong spectacles has sometimes sufficed to cure a person in love." And both men romanticized pain. Berryman, who ought then to have been in his prime, bragged about his frailties in his classes at the University of Minnesota. "I am so weak," he remarked one day, apropos nothing, "that I could not lift that window." On another occasion, he opened a text, looked up, and said, "I hope that I can read this. And if I can't, I shall try another pair of glasses." He took off the glasses he was wearing and fished another pair out of his pocket.

But whatever meaning suffering may have, it is not romantic. It may be inevitable, but it is not inevitably bracing. Whatever destroys me may make me strong, but it may also make me bitter. Unhealed pain may fester like a sore leaving me not strengthened but infected. It may gather like a scab around the emotions, leaving me well-protected but callous. It may breed cynicism, fear, envy, timidity: It is the sickness of unborn pain. And it can kill both the body and the spirit.

This is one possible definition of mental illness: It is the sickness of unborn pain.

Grief

You cannot distract yourself from grief. You cannot dispel it. You cannot conquer it. You can only live through it.

Fear

One day when my twin sister and I were three, our mother was doing the laundry in a gasoline powered washing machine in the yard and our father was clearing and burning brush from the grove that sheltered us from the northern and western winds. My sister and I played while our parents went about their chores. We began to chase each around the bonfire in a game of tag. My sister tripped and fell into the fire. She began to scream horribly. Mother heard the shrieks above the noise of the two-cycle gasoline engine. She turned and saw her daughter engulfed in flames. But she could do nothing. She stood over her laundry tub, unable to emit a sound, to move a muscle, her face contorted in a paroxysm of despair and terror that remains etched into my memory more than half a century later. Father came running from the woods, pulled my sister from the fire and swaddled her in wet clothes. But by then the lower half of her body was already charred.

My sister spent many weeks in the hospital, eventually recovering to the point where she could be indignant about being made to sleep in a crib, and then she came home, heavily bandaged and permanently scarred, but a survivor. My mother, however, never recovered from the deep shame of her helplessness at the critical moment. It was no consolation to her that her paralysis was born of acute fear, not lack of will.

Depression is also a form of fear, and at its deepest, it is also paralytic. It is as useless to ask a person immobilized by depression to summon the power of will as it is to beg a dance of a corpse.

Mind and Soul

Abandonment is what the mind knows. Loss is what the soul knows.

Self-Abandonment

I sat drinking and did not notice the dusk,

Till falling petals filled the folds of my dress.

Drunken I rose and walked to the moonlit stream;

The birds were gone, the men also few.

Li Po

Prayer

What can one say of depression but that it bears the indelible mark of humanity?

Does the mountain brood?

Is the river downcast?

Does the oak tree weep?

Do the ants curse their fate?

Do the fishes of the sea shudder and moan?

Do the grasses of the plains slouch in their places?

No, it is we humans who are cast down and rise again from our travails. You, my Lord, have given to us the sorrows and sighs of the world.

Who am I, oh Lord, to deny your gift?

Beating

When my mother got angry, she selected the nearest child and beat it. Her instrument was a white plastic belt. She applied it to the bare back. There was no use in trying to escape. She always caught you. Crying, or protesting, or twisting to avoid the lashes always made the punishment worse, so you learned not to resist. The belt, which cracked on its descent to flesh, continued to strike until her anger vented. Her anger was seldom satisfied until she had drawn blood. Something about the sight of blood appeased her.

In church, in my teens, when the pastor offered the chalice, saying that it held the blood of Christ, I put my lips to the rim, but I was too terrified to drink.

Disassociation 1

I was six, and I was in the classroom of the one-room country school I attended. The teacher was at the piano. We were playing musical chairs. The teacher began to play, and we students circled around the chairs. When the music stopped, we scrambled for seats. I was left standing. The teacher began to play again. Suddenly, there were two of me. There was the distant little boy moving around the chairs, and there was another me floating up near the ceiling watching the action and paying particular attention to the strange kid with the blond cowlick and the faded overalls. And then I heard a faint voice, which grew louder, until it finally broke through into reality. It was my teacher saying, "Are you all right, Paul? Is anything the matter?" I shook my head and rubbed my eyes, as if I were awaking from a dream. I looked to the ceiling, but no one was there.

"Are you looking for something, Paul?"

"The other boy," I said.

"Which other boy?"

I had no answer.

"Come, sit here. Perhaps you had better have a rest."

That was, I believe, the first symptom of my mental illness.

Disassociation 2

Sometimes a member who wishes to resign from a religious community writes a letter of disassociation. Disassociation in a child is a letter of resignation from the self. It is thought to be brought on by severe physical, sexual, or psychological abuse. In extreme cases, it expresses itself in adults in the form of multiple personalities. This is described in psychiatry as a disorder, but I would say that it is evidence of the miraculous ways by which the spirit is able to survive the intolerable.

The Silver Wagon

I had a silver wagon, a Flying Chief, that went everywhere with me. It was so much a part of me that I dreamed about it. In my sleep I could hear it being pulled around the yard by ghosts. The ghosts lived in the dead hulk of the barkless cottonwood in the corner of the pasture, which took on the same silver color in the moonlight as my wagon. Another favorite possession of mine, for I thought of it as that, was a big granite boulder left behind by a glacier ten thousand years ago, although I did not know that was how it had gotten there. In my household we did not believe in glaciers or evolution or things like that. God made the world six thousand years ago, we believed, just as it is. He handed down his Word in the Elizabethan English of the King James Bible.

One afternoon, for no reason I could have articulated, I decided to smash my silver wagon against the granite boulder. With long running starts, I crashed the wagon against the rock, over and over again. Each crash was more satisfying than the last. I did not stop until the wagon's wheels had come off and its box was full of holes and battered beyond repair. My anger, which had flared to a fine red passion, dissolved in a long moment of trembling, and then emerged in a blissful feeling of peace.

I went to the tool shed, fetched a shovel, and took the remnants of the wagon into the maple grove. I buried them just as if I were burying a pet. I tore off a green maple branch, twisted it into a cross, and set it over the fresh mound of earth. I thought at the time, although I was only seven or eight, that I was burying my childhood.

At supper that evening, my father looked at my mother and then said, "Why did you do that, Paul?" He spoke, for once, more in puzzlement than in rebuke. I shrugged my shoulders. I really didn't know.

"You're not going to get another one, you know."

"I know." I was not regretful. I was past the age of wagons.

Much later, when I was an adult, I would suppose that I was beating my wagon in the same way that I had been beaten, but I knew that this explanation was too simple. The problem I was up against, I think, was one of power: How does a powerless person express great anger? Over and over again, in nations as in children, we have seen the answer: By destroying something, whether it be the self or some symbol of the other, something like the Twin Towers or a silver wagon.

Unreality 1

When sides were chosen in my junior high school gym class, I was always the last boy picked. I was chosen even after the boy who much preferred to sit on the sidelines talking loudly about hair styles and dress design. This was not unfair. I was completely useless to whatever team got stuck with me. But one afternoon I managed to steal the basketball from a kid who had just returned from reform school. The next thing I knew, I was flat on my back on the gym floor, and my nose was gushing blood. The phy ed instructor dispatched me to the nurse's office and sent the reform school boy, who had slugged me, to the principal's office. I could hardly believe my luck. I was out of gym class, that daily hell, half an hour early.

The next afternoon, while my mind was drifting in math class, the thought hit me like Saul's revelation on the road to Damascus: *I ought to have hit him back!* Even then, I was not moved by any desire to avenge my attacker, or to defend myself. Because my body was not real to me, it hardly mattered who took a punch at it or what damage was done. I realized, further, that this would have been the socially correct thing for a boy to do. How were boys supposed to behave? I had no idea. I was an alien in an unreal world, a being entirely composed of thoughts, trying to make his way among creatures brimming out of their bodies. I was desperate not to be found out, and certain that the game was already up.

Unreality 2

Our training in basketball in the seventh grade consisted solely of a series of scrimmages played while the gym teacher read paperback novels. I knew no more about basketball than I did about Greek belly dancing. There were no rules about giving players equal time, so I had spent no more than ten minutes on the court when the scrimmages came to an end and we were given our test. While the rest of the class sat in the bleachers, we were sent out one at a time to dribble up and down the court twice, making layups at either end. These maneuvers were timed.

I watched the first couple of boys to find out what a layup *was*. It was something, I saw, that I had never attempted. I had never tried to dribble a basketball either. I prayed that I might be granted sudden death. The inevitable, however, happened. My turn was called. I went to the center of the vast court with the ball in my hands. "Start!" the teacher called. I tried to dribble, lost control of the ball, ran after it, tried again. And again. And again. The boys in the bleachers began to titter. In desperation, I threw the ball ahead of myself, and ran to catch it, and did so over and over until I reached the basket. My shot did not touch the backboard. I tried several times more. Finally, making no pretense at a layup, I managed, standing flat on my feet, to get the ball through the basket. I turned to run the gauntlet to the opposite basket.

Now my classmates were roaring with laughter, which got all the more hysterical the farther I advanced down the court. I neared the basket. The ball got away from me. I ran out into the auditorium to fetch it. As I was returning to the court, I saw the source of the merriment. My teacher was standing on the sidelines imitating me.

40

I tried several times, halfheartedly, to get the ball into the basket, then gave up and started down the court again. By then my classmates had joined the teacher in mocking imitations of my performance. They were not just laughing; they were hooting and screaming and pounding each other on the back and doubling over in pained hilarity. I crossed the center line. Then I picked up the ball, walked to my teacher, and handed it to him. I took my place again on the bleachers.

I was hurt, but not embarrassed. I had no reason to be embarrassed. That boy out on the basketball court was not me. If you had shown me a home movie of him in action, I would not have recognized him. I would have thought he was funny, too. You couldn't poke fun at the real me, who was not made of flesh and blood and did not dribble basketballs.

It would be a very long time before I came to see that the boy who dribbled basketballs badly really was me. By then the long years of sequestration in the ethereal self had taken a terrible toll.

Life hurls us like a stone, and we sail through the air saying, "Look at me move."

FERNANDO PESSOA

Love 1

I was madly in love, when I was six, with a girl named Elia Jean. We went to the same country school. At recess, we smooched in the road ditch. Or, while the other children played, we rehearsed the wedding march. We fully intended to be married. We had to settle, in the meantime, though, for our own private club, which met, as often as possible, in the cupola of her parents' round barn.

Elia Jean's sister was rabidly jealous of our club. She insisted that she be included as a member. She taunted us. She told her mother lies about us to get us into trouble. But we steadfastly refused her pleas. One day we quarreled with her yet again about our club. We told her to get lost. She ran to the house, crying. Elia Jean and I headed, hand in hand, for the barn. Her sister, still crying, stuck her head out the window of her room. "Pigs!" she screamed. "Dirty rotten pigs!" and then the window crashed down on her neck. She had to go to the hospital.

That was the day I learned the connection between love and guilt.

Love 2

I had my second breakdown when my son was thirteen or fourteen. It became part of my routine during that time to take my evening medications and then to sit in the living room and listen to music until the sleeping pills took effect. This went on for two or three months. Every evening, after I had started the music, my son came and sat on the couch beside me. He said nothing. Given my mood at the time, the effort would have been futile. He did not look at me or touch me. He simply sat there with me. When I began to get sleepy, I wished him a good night and went to my bedroom. He went back to his studies.

There have been hundreds of nights since when I, in a black mood, have felt, even though he was thousands of miles away, the comfort of his company.

Love 3

During my sophomore year in college, I shared an apartment with a man who was a couple years older than I. He was ruggedly handsome. He reminded me of James Dean and the young Marlon Brando, whom he worshipped. He wore white tee shirts and Levis and had intense brown eyes and a shy grin. He angled cigarettes out of the corner of his mouth, after the manner of the film stars, and drank gin. He was a man of great enthusiasms: Bob Dylan, Italian food, Pancho Villa, William Gladstone, George Orwell. When he got interested in something or someone, he set out to learn everything he could on the subject, and his talk about what he had discovered was mesmerizing.

Like me, he was an aspiring writer. He was otherwise everything I was not. He was worldly, sophisticated, endlessly jovial. I admired everything about him and wanted to be like him in every way. He seemed an older brother. I became interested in politics, read Orwell, listened to Dylan, took up the drinking of gin and smoking of cigarettes, saw *On the Waterfront.*

We took care of each other. He educated me, talked me out of my moods, and elevated my tastes. He was, however, domestically incompetent. Alarm clocks didn't waken him. I got him up in the morning. To the extent that we cooked, I did it. I cleaned. I showed him practical things, like how to use a can opener. His mother came by every week to do his laundry. I did mine. Sometimes I went home with him weekends. His parents became my parents.

The part of our relationship that I liked most was that, after the lights were out at night and we had gone to bed, we talked, sometimes for hours. He had a low, lovely voice which soothed me and drew me out of myself. We talked about everything: our friends, our ambitions, national affairs, the reading and writing we were doing, college life, our parents, our siblings, music, food, memories, regrets, hopes. On nights when he came in late, I waited up for him. I couldn't sleep without hearing his voice.

One night after we had gone to bed, he said, in a tone I didn't recognize, "There's something I have to tell you, Paul."

"I'm all ears."

He hesitated. "Well the thing is," he said, "my girlfriend and I had a baby today. I'm getting married." I was stunned. I didn't know that he had a girlfriend, much less one who was pregnant. So that's where he had been all those nights. We talked about his beautiful daughter. He asked me to be the best man at his wedding. He told me that the wedding and his departure from our apartment were to take place in two weeks.

I don't know how I got through the next two weeks and the wedding. I remember nothing at all about that time. After the wedding, he, his wife and baby, and I went back to the apartment. He gave me a hug and then got back into the car and drove away. I went in, collapsed on my bed, and cried bitterly for hours.

Except to go out now and then to the corner store for a package of hot dogs, the only thing I ate, I stayed in the apartment for the next two months. I slept for days at a time. I developed a stubborn fever. I vomited repeatedly. I bled from the nose and the anus. I cried. I thought about suicide. I flunked all my classes. And then, somehow, I got over it and returned to life. My former roommate graduated, and I found new ones. I fell in love with my wife-to-be.

The possibilities for self-blindness are infinite. I did not know until twenty years later that I had been, and still was, in love with that man. I still am.

Love 4

For several years my wife and I made foster homes for a number of teenaged girls who had been abused by their parents. Several of them had been raped by their fathers. The most severely traumatized of the girls had been sexually assaulted by a progression of her mother's boyfriends. She had been beaten hard enough to break bones. She had been locked alone in her house, often for days at a time, while her mother went off on drunken binges. Sometimes she had been left with nothing to eat. She had been mercilessly teased and harassed at school because she wore men's clothing, did not bathe or comb her hair or use deodorant, and had become morbidly obese. She was, moreover, mildly retarded. When she came to us, she was so defeated in spirit that she had ceased to function, on almost any level, as a human being. Ours was the sixth or seventh foster home in which she had been placed. Nobody knew what to do with her. We did our best, and the girl made some progress while she lived with us. Her intense and random hostility eased. Her violent temper tantrums, which were frightening because of her size, grew fewer in number. She lost eighty pounds, began to take better care of herself, went to a summer camp for girls who had, like her, been savagely abused, and she found a friend there, her first. But after a year we were utterly exhausted and concerned that, in our efforts to meet her needs, we were neglecting our own children. So with heavy hearts, we said goodbye to her one morning and she was taken away to an institution.

Darlene, as I shall call her, may have endured more pain than a child can bear. Some people survive and prosper, for reasons we don't understand, and some don't. I don't know about Darlene. I lost track of her years ago. But even in the extremity of her abuse, she shared three traits with the rest of our foster children. She knew that she had suffered and was miserable, for one thing, but she had absolutely no sense that she had been *abused*. She assumed, as all of the girls did, that this was the way of life for children, that nothing that had happened to her was at all out of the ordinary. It did not occur to her to talk about her life with others because she did not know that it was remarkable. She assumed, for another thing, that to the extent that she had suffered, she had deserved it, that the fault lay in her, not in her abusers. And she passionately, loyally, unconditionally loved her abusers.

It is this last fact that appalls me and moves me at the same time. It speaks, on the one hand, to how completely vulnerable children really are. But it also testifies to the invincible power of love. Child-love is angel-love. It is the almighty love of God. If we adults appreciated how little we have done to earn it, and how much of it we have been given, the world would be a vastly different place.

My Grandmother's Laughter

My grandmother was not religious, but she kept a plaque above her dining table that read, "Earth hath no sorrow that Heaven cannot cure." Anyone who led a life as spare as my grandmother's would be bound to believe in Heaven. One morning when she was a young woman, she got married. That afternoon, she returned to her work as a washer-woman. She may not have had a real day's rest after that until she was old. Even in old age, she could not keep still; she made it her full-time occupation to know the neighbors' business. By rubbering on the party telephone line, keeping watch from her windows on the movements of the traffic, and using her well-developed powers of deduction (her favorite television program was *The Alfred Hitchcock Hour*), she pretty much knew all there was to know about the neighbors. She was happy to report her findings to anyone who would listen. She lived in the days when rural newspapers still had gossip columns. Except for the problem of libel, she would have made a first-rate reporter.

Sometimes it happens that a person who has almost nothing (my grandparents were farmers for half a century without acquiring a single acre of land) is content to make do with even less. Marvelous aromas wafted from my grandmother's kitchen when she was cooking. Then, at the last minute, she doused everything in boiling water so that it came to the table bereft of all flavor. Often, in old age, my grandparents made an evening meal of a glass of milk and a canned pear or peach apiece. I can think of only two extravagances in my grandmother's life. One was her snore. When I hear the fog horns in Duluth, I am reminded of the nights when I slept over at her house.

The other was my grandmother's laugh, which was big, boisterous, and frequent. My grandmother found funny things funny, but, to her, tragic things were also occasions for laughter. She laughed at funerals. She laughed when people were maimed in accidents. One day our house caught fire. My mother telephoned my grandmother to ask her to tell my father, who was working at his parents' place, to come

49

home right away. My grandmother laughed and laughed at the news, forever offending her daughter-in-law. A woman schooled in poverty and experienced in burying her children, my grandmother did not laugh at adversity because she found it funny. She laughed because there was nothing else she could do, and because it was easier to laugh than to cry.

I sometimes tell this story to people who say to me, "How can you be depressed? I see you laughing all the time."

My father, by the way, did not come home until he had finished his plowing hours later. My mother was, quite rightly, furious. He was baffled by her fury. One need not forgive him to understand him. He, like his mother before him, was schooled in poverty. When you are poor, you learn the bitter way that there are a great many things you cannot change, and that the path of survival lies in not even trying. Sometimes you just have to laugh.

Revelations

How I learned that my mother was, like me, mentally ill:

I was in the kitchen cooking dinner for my family. I could not find the particular spoon I wanted. I rummaged through several drawers, cursing loudly as I hunted, my irritation steadily mounting. I got to the last of the drawers that the spoon might be in. It was not there. Suddenly, startling even myself, I pulled all of the drawers off their runners, one after another, and dumped their contents onto the floor. The spoon I had been searching for stared up at me out of the rubble. As quickly as my rage had flared, it abated. Feeling miserable and ashamed, I put the drawers back in their places and picked up and replaced the utensils. I went on with the meal.

It was then that I remembered an evening when I stood, still a small boy, in our kitchen and watched as my mother prepared to set the table for supper. She opened a cupboard door. A plate fell out and shattered on the floor. I ran to hide, because I already knew the meaning of my mother's moods. From the living room I heard her take out every other plate, one at a time, and hurl it to the floor. After the plates came the saucers and the cups, everything broken beyond repair. And then my mother rushed past me and into the bedroom. I heard her weeping. She wept for ten minutes. She emerged with a grim smile pasted on her face. She got the broom and dustpan, swept up the shards of glass, and threw them away. Then she served supper in soup bowls, the only items of dinnerware we had left. We ate in complete silence, except for the table prayer. No one even looked at anybody else.

I finally got help for my illness and, on medication, found that my bursts of rage gradually ended. I realized that they had been a part of my illness, and of my mother's illness, too. A dozen years passed. One night I got to thinking about those two incidents, and I noticed, for the first time, that I was always alone in the kitchen when I cooked dinner, and that the meals, although they were very good, never seemed to evoke any satisfaction in my family. My wife and my children, I suddenly knew, had hidden from me just as my sisters and I had hidden from our mother. They were *afraid* of me. I had been a raving madman.

I had never felt such deep sorrow. I had not cried since the night my father died, twenty years previously. I cried all that night, and all the next day, and all the next night. If only you could relive your life. If only it were possible to repair your life. In a week or so, I mentioned this discovery to my therapist. I had been in therapy for a dozen years and had never once cried, but now I found myself sobbing and could not stop. I heard a strange keening sound coming from my mouth.

I went home and wrote a letter of deep apology to my estranged wife, for that sin and for all the others that I was not aware of yet.

I never got a reply.

Some sins are not forgivable, at least not on this earth, and not by mere mortals. There are some sins you are condemned to live with until the end of your natural time.

Work 1

One day when I was about twelve, my father asked me to take the tractor from our farm to my grandparents' place. This was a trip of four or five miles on country roads. The tractor was a little Fordson. It had a top running speed of five or six miles an hour. There was not much to operating it. You pushed in the clutch, pulled down the gear lever, let out the clutch, and the machine lurched forward. Then you opened the throttle and you were on your way. But what a glorious way it was! I sat on the iron seat of that machine, both hands firmly gripping the wheel, and drove down our long driveway and out into the world. I was making my debut as a working man. Not that I hadn't done plenty of work before, but this was different. This was not a child's work. This was a *man's* work. I proceeded as if I were on my way to the United States capitol to be inaugurated. I waved at every passing truck and car, waved to herds of cattle, waved at every farmstead, whether anyone was visible or not. I wished to be noticed. I had made my way in the life. I was employed! When I arrived at my grandparents' farm, you couldn't have told me from Arnold Schwarzenegger.

Looking back now, I can see that there have been four supremely happy days in my life: the day I was married, the day my daughter was born, the day my son was born, and the day I first took to the road on that Fordson. Love, children and work: all the rest is incidental.

Work 2

John Berryman once said, correctly, that the most beautiful verse in the Bible is, *Come unto me all ye who labor and are heavy laden, and I will give you rest.* There are many ideas in this verse, but the one that particularly interests me, as someone who has not seriously labored for three years, is that labor and rest are necessarily connected. Labor gives meaning to rest, and rest gives meaning to labor. In the absence of one, the possibility of the other does not exist. We need work, and rest from work, as much as the body needs a heart.

My own workless days and nights pass in a numbing blur. Morning is indistinguishable from evening. One week passes into the next. I remember nothing because there is nothing to remember. I eat, not because I'm hungry, but because the clock says it's time to eat. I sometimes sleep eighteen or twenty hours a day, but I am always tired. There is no rest. I take my pills at eight a.m., four p.m., and ten p.m. The remainder of my time is without form or structure. Days when I have an appointment with a doctor stand out because then I have something to do. I remember, then, to shower, brush my teeth, put on clean clothes, activities that most days seem as pointless as the days themselves. I used to work eighteen or twenty hours a day. These days, I can't imagine how I did it. Of course, when I was working I couldn't have imagined spending so much time in bed.

If you are a madman, what is your work?

Disability

My biggest mistake was in allowing myself to be called disabled. When I did so, I became, in my own mind, disabled. And once that happened, I *was* disabled. I defined myself by what I couldn't do. But the number of things I could do was far greater. I subtracted three from ten and got minus thirteen. It was bad arithmetic no matter how you look at it.

Work 3

A friend observes that every depressed person he knows is struggling with a major vocational issue.

Work 4

If I had learned to take pleasure in the work, I would have been satis-fied with its outcome.

Work does not imply success. It implies work, which has a sufficient beauty.

Parents: An Interview

Did you have good parents? I did.

What did they do for you? They gave us the foundation of their deep religious belief. They taught us to believe in hard work and personal responsibility. They tried to show us by example how to accept fate without complaint. Because they both worked at home, they were a constant presence in our lives. They loved us.

Did they make mistakes? Certainly. Don't all parents?

For example? I wish that my father's approval had been as vigorous as his rebukes. I wish that my mother had not beaten us. I wish that the religious faith we were given had not been so dour.

Have these mistakes shaped your life? No. But they've influenced it.

In what way? I suppose the most important thing is that I have been trying all my life to earn the approval I didn't get from my father. Stupid, of course, toxic, futile. And when we were raising our own children, I tried, like everyone, not to repeat my parents' mistakes.

Did you succeed in that? I don't know. You'd have to ask my children. I suppose I created my own variations on my parents' mistakes.

Say more. I didn't beat my children, but I was as wrathful in other ways. I tried to praise my children, but I was as perfectionist as my father.

Do you think your struggles with depression are explained by the parenting you had? No. I think about my own children when I say that. I believe that we raised both of them in approximately the same way. They grew up in the same household. They were equally subjected, so far as I know, to our flaws and our strengths. Both are extremely bright and resourceful adults. One of them is emotionally well-balanced and goal oriented. The other struggled emotionally.

So emotional difficulties are a matter of innate personality? That might have something to do with it. But again I consider my own children. The one who was well-balanced was a kid who would eat only cold baked beans for lunch, insisted on wearing a snow suit in July, and had from the beginning a fierce resistance to authority of any kind. The one who struggled was a serene baby and a warm and vivacious child. Who knows what goes wrong?

It's a matter of genes, then? Twin studies do suggest that there is a genetic factor in mental illness, but most people who would seem to be genetically vulnerable do just fine. To the extent that genes are at work, there have to be triggers that activate them. Nobody knows what those are.

So where does this leave parents? Right where they started. Nobody is adequately prepared to be a parent. You do the best you can. Hang on when the bad times come. Laugh. Pray.

Madness, at its core, is a condition of profound solitude.

SILKE-MARIA WEINECK

Have you ever seen a severed hand or foot, or a decapitated head,
just lying somewhere far away from the body it belonged to? . . . That's what
we do to ourselves—or try to—when we rebel against what happens to us,
when we segregate ourselves. Or when we do something selfish.

MARCUS AURELIUS

Suicide 1

To the healthy person, suicide seems not only unconscionable but unfathomable. But to someone seized by deep depression, the thought of suicide, or more abstractly, of death, may appear logical and morally compelling. In dying, such a person thinks, I will relieve the world of my misery, and also of the misery of those who are made miserable by my misery. Such thoughts may be life-saving.

I have managed, on thousands of nights, to fall asleep and so to make it from one day to the next only by assuring myself that I might well die before morning in the natural course of things, and that I could always, should the pain become absolutely unbearable, take matters into my own hands. In doing so I have fought against the impulsive nature of suicide in two ways: by holding out the possibility that relief will arrive of its own accord, and by raising the bar for action: only when the pain becomes *absolutely* unbearable. I have often kept the means of suicide within reach of my bed. It has comforted me to have them there. And they have been a practical argument against immediate action: you can afford to wait a bit, I tell myself, because everything is already prepared. I do so even now, when I am writing and thinking again for the first time in three years.

Suicide, when it happens, is often, although I think not inevitably, tragic, but the *thought* of suicide might well be a successful adaptation of the human mind to extreme emotional distress. I have wondered what would happen if mental health professionals were to treat "suicide ideation," as they call it, making it bloodless and abstract, as a tool and not as a threat.

The possibility of suicide is a common, and often daily, presence in the lives of people suffering severe depression. If you talk about this, however, you get sent to the hospital, which is like being sent to jail. So in the mental health system as it now operates, patients quickly learn to keep their suicidal thoughts to themselves. What if patients felt free to talk openly about these thoughts and were given guidance in how to use them to ward off rather than to accomplish death? That would mean, of course, that caregivers would have to feel free to talk realistically about suicide, and not just to repeat the same old cautionary bromides that every suicidal patient has heard a hundred times—suicide is a permanent solution to a temporary problem, and so on. I have no idea what it would take to bring that about.

Suicide 2

My last attempt at suicide occurred nearly two years ago. In the time since, my friends and relatives have been careful not to broach the subject with me. They came to visit my wife in the days after it appeared likely that I would survive, but they did not stop at the hospital to see me. Only a week ago, I learned that my adult children had not been told that I had tried to kill myself. This makes me sad for their mother, who could have used their help.

Once, I myself raised the subject with an old friend.

"So how about them Twins?" she replied.

After an attempted suicide, you become aware of yourself again one morning and discover that you have not died after all; you have merely become invisible.

Suicide 3

What exactly is the difference between a man who sacrifices his life in a pointless war out of a mistaken sense of duty to his country and a man who sacrifices his life by suicide in the mistaken belief that doing so will improve the lives of those he loves? In the matter of foolish sacrifices, where lies the dividing point between honor and perfidy, recklessness and principle?

Suicide 4

One man shoots and kills another. We do not say of him that he was being selfish; we say that he is a murderer. Another man runs a red light, striking and killing a pedestrian. We do not say of the driver that he was acting selfishly; we say that he committed homicide. A dictator orders the execution of his opponents. We say that he is a tyrant. The president of one nation sends his troops to attack another. We say that he is a hero or a villain, depending upon the circumstances and our loyalties. A man takes his own life. While we may believe that the man was committing a crime or a sin, what we say is that he was behaving very selfishly.

Pointing out the selfishness in suicide can be an effective deterrent against it. I myself, when I have felt suicidal, have (usually) not acted because that was not the legacy I wanted to leave to my children, and because I had friends who might have been tempted to take my death as an example. But to describe suicide in terms of selfishness is profoundly to trivialize it. It puts suicide in a category with not sharing on the playground or refusing to give up your seat on the bus to an old woman.

It is hard to see how life has any meaning at all if it is not to be taken as sacred, in and of itself, without reference to any other consideration. Unless we believe that life is neither ours to give or to take, unless we hold life as the fundamental miracle, as something absolutely inviolate, we condemn ourselves to existence in a perpetual state of terror. We could never, otherwise, be safe, either from ourselves or from any other human being.

That is why I join with fundamentalists in abhorring most abortions and part ways with them in also abhorring all wars, capital punishment, the abuse of ecosystems, and the accumulation of great personal wealth: every kind of lethality. The full expression of human life depends upon two fundamental conditions, peace and justice, which presently exist nowhere on earth.

But who are you to talk? I ask myself, even as I hear you asking the same question. It is true. I tried to kill myself. I was disappointed when I did not succeed. I have only two responses: to offer my confession: I am guilty of the most grievous of sins; and, to pray that I might make the rest of my life an atonement.

Suicide 5

A young intellectually competent woman I know was committed to a locked nursing home for patients with dementia. She spent a day there. Most of the staff, she said, barely spoke English, and they were cruel to their patients. She decided she couldn't bear to spend her life in such a place. So she went to her room, broke a bottle, and stabbed herself. Then she tore up a bed sheet and attempted to hang herself on the bathroom door. While she was in the act, a staff member came into her room.

"Just remember," the aide said, "when you're dead, I'll still be alive."

Suicide 6

I was battling the impulse to commit suicide. I spent a few days in the hospital until the urge subsided. The next time I saw my therapist, he said, "I was really worried about you. I was tempted to call you. But I talked to —— (a nurse who had not seen me in a year), and she said, "I wouldn't worry about him. He goes through these moods, but he always manages to pull himself out of it. He's a survivor."

The next week I wrote the therapist a letter. "I have one earnest request," I wrote. "Please don't ever tell somebody like me that he or she is merely toying with suicide. I spent four terrible days after I left your office the last time battling the powerful urge to kill myself just to prove how mistaken you (and ——) were. The next time, somebody could die. In fact, I've never made a suicidal gesture in my life. I don't slash my wrists or abrade my arms or burn cigarette holes in my thighs or take fifteen pills and call the police. I have been saved by the days I've spent in intensive care wards, and the next time I will not fail."

I never got a response.

An Explanation

I don't know why my therapist didn't respond to my letter, but he had three good reasons not to.

First, therapy occurs in a relationship, in a real time encounter between two persons. My letter was not an attempt to extend that relationship. It was a move to circumvent it by getting in the last word.

Second, I couched my complaint in an expression of concern for others, but my real concern was for my own wounded pride. The letter was, therefore, deceitful.

Third, the letter contains an explicit threat: I am going to kill myself. And it contains an implicit accusation: When I do, it will be your fault. It is, therefore, an attempt at blackmail.

None of these violations of my relationship with my therapist was conscious. That is, I did not sit down with the intention of one-upping my therapist, lying to him, or blackmailing him. At the time, I thought I was being helpful. But I routinely poison relationships by employing such behaviors. Then, when the relationships falter, I get depressed. Do I get depressed because I have bad brain chemistry? Do I get depressed because I am forced to face the consequences of my contemptible behavior? Or do I get depressed in order to escape the consequences of my bad behavior: Don't blame me; I'm sick?

The psychiatrist Thomas S. Szasz would choose the latter explanation. In *The Myth of Mental Illness* he argues that mental illness is a language, not a disease. To treat it as a disease, he argues, is to take the patient off the hook, to give the patient a legitimate reason for behaving self-destructively. A moral therapy, he says, would help the patient to understand his own language and, in doing so, to give him a choice. Do I wish to continue to speak this language, or do I want to find a more effective way of expressing my pain?

I believe that Szasz is correct.

Suicide 7

The desire to commit suicide is not an action. It is an expression. It says, roughly, "Help!" To claim, therefore that some suicidal thinking is authentic and some is not is to engage in a *non sequitur*. It makes no sense to say, "That's not true" to someone who cries "Help!" It is like replying, "That's not a cabbage" to someone who has said, "I love dogs." Even when the cry, "Help!" is manipulative, the plea itself is real. The therapeutic response to such a plea is to seek the source of the pain and to try to find a way to end it. The conventional psychiatric response, however, is to try to find a drug that will mask the pain. This is like throwing a drowning person a tranquilizer rather than a safety ring. Too often, the psychotherapeutic response is to ask, "What is your motive for telling me this?" When a person cries, "Help! I'm drowning!" the lifeguard does not yell back, "Can you tell me why you feel that way?" He dives to the rescue.

Suicide 8

Suicide is so repugnant because it raises the possibility that we don't *need* to live.

It doesn't bother you that you only weigh x or y pounds and not three hundred. Why should it bother you more that you have only x or y years to live and no more? You accept the limits placed on your body. Accept those placed on your time.

MARCUS AURELIAS

Death

A woman has occupied a living corpse for a dozen years. Her husband believes that she would not have wanted to survive in this way. Few people would. Her parents accuse her husband of wanting to resume his own existence. They are willing to hold his potentially beneficial life hostage to her machine-assisted one. Some say the husband is selfish, but no one makes the same charge against the parents. A legislature and a governor rush to their assistance. The governor orders that the woman's feeding tube be reinserted. Some say that this affirms the right to life. I say that it affirms the right to delusions.

It is an odd fact that in the history of humanity that we have been dying for millennia, without exception, and yet we still cannot face the fact that this is not a tragedy.

It doesn't matter how good a life you've led. There'll still be people standing around the bed who will welcome the sad event.

MARCUS AURELIUS

Prayer

Forgive me, Lord.

I thought You owed me a lifetime of laughter.

I thought You owed me prosperity.

I thought You owed me adulation.

I thought You owed me protection from pain.

I thought You owed me freedom from sin.

I thought You owed me pity.

But You gave me the seas and the stars.

You gave me thunderstorms and hail.

You gave me the cleansing rain of tears.

You gave me sleep.

You gave me the dawn.

You gave me imperfection and absolved me of it.

You gave me life.

Forgive me, Lord, for receiving your gifts with closed eyes and a hard heart. Open my eyes and soften my heart, O Lord. Grant me the vulnerability of grace to the end of my days.

The Hospital 1

This is the acute-care psychiatric ward, at the turn of the 21st century. You enter through a locked door that opens onto a small entryway. There you give up your shoes and everything that is in your pockets. They will be returned to you when you are discharged. Then you are ushered through a second locked door onto the ward itself. No matter how many times you have made this entrance, you are frightened. There is no telling what might happen to you in the days ahead.

A nurse comes out of an office encased in thick, unbreakable Plexiglas. The door to the office is always locked. The nurse leads you to a small examination room. She takes your blood pressure and your temperature. Then she asks you to disrobe. You hesitate when you've gotten down to your boxers. "I'm sorry but you'll have to remove your shorts, too," she says. You stand naked before her. She inspects you for signs of contraband. "You may pull up your shorts." The nurse issues you a pair of pajamas and a pair of hospital socks, the standard uniform. The pajamas generally seem to be either puke green or baby blue. The socks have grippers on the soles. They will serve as shoes for the duration of your stay. The clothes you came in wearing are taken away. The last time you wore pajamas twenty-four hours a day, you were an infant. You have now assumed the appearance of a mental patient.

You are led down a long hallway to your room. The hallway is wide and barren. The room has two beds, a window, and one hard, low-backed chair. The window is covered in thick Plexiglas. The floor is hard and the walls are unornamented. Everything is some shade of gray. The beds are standard hospital issue. The mattresses are two or three inches thick and vinyl covered. There are thin, roughly textured sheets and a flimsy blanket that will not keep you warm. It is always chilly in psychiatric wards. The pillow is child-sized, perhaps an inch thick, and covered in noisy plastic. The beds have rails. There is a plain vanity between them but no lamp. Except for the chair, nothing in the room is portable. There is a sink and above it a metal (unbreakable) mirror. In a strong light you can see yourself in it dimly. The bathroom has a stool and a shower with a flimsy plastic curtain. The curtain rod is designed to collapse should you try to hang yourself on it. The shower operates with a push button that produces a thirty-second burst of water at a preset temperature. In order to complete a shower, you have to push the button repeatedly. The bathroom locks with a key from the outside only. If you are considered a suicide risk, it will stay locked. Should you need to use the bathroom, you will have to go down the hall to the nurses' station, knock on the window, and ask for permission to use it.

You are issued supplies: a motel-room-sized bar of soap, a sample size bottle of Johnson & Johnson baby shampoo, a tiny tube of toothpaste, and a comb and toothbrush, both of the cheapest kind. There are also a towel and a washcloth. Both are thin enough to see through. If you have three of the towels, it is possible to dry off after a shower.

The door to your room does not lock. It has a small window in it, through which you can be checked, if you are suicidal, every fifteen minutes, twenty-four hours a day.

Down the hallway, next to the nursing station, there is a day room. It is furnished with tables that have been bolted down and with hard plastic chairs, also unmovable. There is a television set that runs all day at an inescapable volume. On a shelf, there are a few paperback romance novels. There is also a single telephone on which you may receive and make calls. Unless you have a calling card, which few of the patients do, the outgoing calls must be local. If you are a patient from out of town, you are out of luck.

Until your doctor decides otherwise, this is home.

The Hospital 2

This is the hospital routine.

Early in the morning, usually just after you have finally managed to fall asleep, your doctor visits you for four or five minutes. At 7:30 a nurse comes around to take your temperature and blood pressure. At 7:45 meds are distributed. At 8:00, there is breakfast.

Mid-morning, something called occupational therapy is offered for an hour or so. Usually this consists of doing the sort of craft or art project you last attempted in kindergarten. It has never been clear to me in what respect this activity is either occupational or therapeutic. I always skip it.

Lunch at noon. If you consult the menu, you can usually identify the tasteless gray blobs on your tray. These are eaten with plastic spoons and forks.

Afternoon meds are distributed at 4:30.

At 5:00 p.m. there is another mysterious meal.

7:30: Temps and blood pressures again.

8:00: More meds.

10:00: Lights are dimmed.

During the day, you can knock at the nurse's station door on the hour and ask for a tepid cup of decaffeinated coffee, a soda, a nicotine patch.

All the rest of the time is yours. You have three options: you can sleep, you can watch television, or you can pace the hallway. Sometimes a game is made of pacing. You call out the rounds as you pass a fellow in-mate, or you pretend you are walking across the country and announce the name of the city you've just been through, or you march in tandem. This is recorded in the nursing notes as "pacing behavior." If you watch this activity, you can't help being reminded of zoo animals in their cages.

Three or four days of this routine and you are bored to the bones.

Boredom 1

The world of the mentally ill is replete with boredom. You have nothing to think about except yourself. And you have nothing to talk about except your illness.

Boredom 2

Babies have pacifiers. Adults have television. The reason the television set is in the center of the psychiatric ward life is that watching it is the only thing in life that requires less effort than sleeping.

Boredom 3

One reason why people are so afraid of the mentally ill is that we are so unbearably boring. Staying awake through a psychotic monologue or the lamentations of a depressed person is one of the hardest labors a human being can undertake. Why otherwise apparently intelligent therapists volunteer to do this day after day, year after year, is one of life's great mysteries. The slightest sign of curiosity in a patient must be as momentous to a therapist as the first ray of sunshine to a man who has been chained in a dungeon for seven years.

The Hospital 3

Taken together, the environment and the routine of the psychiatric ward are known in the trade as "the therapeutic milieu." Reduce an adult to the status of a child, put him in surroundings that resemble as little as possible a home, deprive him of nearly all intellectual and sensory stimuli, induce nicotine and caffeine withdrawal, and provoke a simultaneous state of insomnia and intense boredom. Perhaps there is something therapeutic in this, but I confess that I cannot see what it is. Of course, I am not a psychiatrist.

The Hospital 4

There are rare moments of drama on a pysch ward, all of them upsetting.

Sometimes a new inmate will be delivered or taken away by the police. On these occasions the patient will be handcuffed and chained at the ankles, and the entrance or departure will be accompanied by the rattling of the chains, which echoes against the hard surfaces of the ward. It is always depressing to see one of your own being treated like a wild animal.

Occasionally a patient will have a violent or manic outburst. Someone on the staff triggers a button and a voice comes on the intercom, saying over and over again, "Tech alert. Tech alert. Tech alert." The burliest nurses and aides rush to the scene, wrestle the patient into submission, and inject a dose of Haldol and a minor tranquilizer. Sometimes the patient is hustled off to a seclusion room and strapped by the wrists, ankles, and waist to a bed. Every effort is made to keep the rest of the patients out of sight while this is unfolding, but we know only too well what is going on. Anyway, we can see the restrained patient later through the half-opened door in which sits the tech assigned to keep constant watch. I think one's sympathy is always for the patient.

Occasionally one will have a run-in with a nurse. I got up one night, at one of the state hospitals that still allows cigarettes, and asked if I could go to the smoking room.

"No." the nurse said curtly.

I was furious but held my tongue. I knew I was within my rights, but I was being transferred to a private hospital the next day, and I didn't want to mess that up. I stood and stared at the man. My roommate came to the desk, too. I had apparently awakened him. "May I have a smoke?" he asked.

"Sure," the nurse said. "Go right ahead."

"I'd like to have a smoke," I said, struggling mightily to hold in my temper.

He looked at me and smiled. "One person at a time," he said.

I glared at him.

"Look it up. It's in the rules."

I waited until my roommate had finished his cigarette.

"Now may I have a cigarette?" I asked

"Of course. I didn't know you wanted to *smoke*."

I had my cigarette, fuming all the while.

On my way back to my room, I paused at the nursing desk.

The nurse looked up. "Yes?" he said, smiling sweetly.

"Have you always been an asshole?"? I said.

That was the start of a series of events that led to my spending the rest of the night in the seclusion room. I was actually grateful to be there. My roommate's snore rattled the furniture. For once I got a night's sleep. And it was a change of scenery.

Sometimes it is the other patients you have to look out for. One day when I was still new to psych wards, I walked up to the dayroom window to look outside. There was another patient at the window. He turned instantly and snarled, "Stop staring at me!"

"I wasn't staring," I said "I just wanted to look out the window."

"Stay away from my window!"

"Sorry. I didn't know you owned the window."

And then he was at my throat. A nurse came to my rescue.

As he was being led away, the patient turned and hissed, "Just remember, I own your sorry ass."

And he did. I made it a point never to be in the same room with him again.

The Hospital 5

Suppose that you never knew privacy. Suppose that you were being watched all the time, waking or sleeping. Suppose that the people who watched you were making notes about what they saw, notes to which you were not privy. Suppose that everything you did or said, or didn't do or didn't say, was assumed to be a manifestation of some sickness in your mind. Suppose you knew that these notes were being entered into the permanent record of your life.

If you can imagine that, you can begin to imagine what it is like to be a patient on a psychiatric ward at the beginning of the 21st century.

The Hospital 6

A great deal of thought has been given, in the design of hospital psychiatric wards, to matters of safety and security. They are, so far as this is possible, suicide-safe. Windows are impenetrable, lights are recessed, doors are lockable only by the staff, hallways are wide enough so that disruptive actions by patients can be easily managed, anything that might be used as a weapon is bolted down, floor plans are arranged so that staff can easily observe patients at all times, procedures for the use of restraints are carefully spelled out, mechanical controls and switches are locked in cages, drugs are securely stored, packages intended for patients are carefully searched, visitors are screened for contraband. Nothing affecting security and safety seems to have been overlooked.

But no thought at all, so far as I have been able to determine, has been given to what might make these wards healing places. I searched more than a thousand Internet sites, the indexes of two hundred books on psychiatric hospital design and management, and various standards for accreditation. My search yielded one relevant document, a set of guidelines in New Zealand for the construction of new psychiatric hospitals. The commission that wrote these guidelines reported that its own search of the literature had come up short.

"Essentially," the New Zealand commission wrote, "facilities are for the benefit of the people who use them and must enhance their sense of dignity and comfort while promoting autonomy and ensuring safety. The onus is on all who participate in the design and building process to understand the end uses of the facility and to recognize and respect the needs of future occupants. Often the best way to insure this is to involve people with service user experience in planning and design."

With that goal in mind, the commission suggested that:

There should be one activity space for every two patients.

To protect the needs of women, there should be spaces where they can be by themselves.

To protect the needs of cultural minorities, there should be spaces that allow them to observe their own social customs.

There should be indoor exercise space.

There should be a separate space to meet the needs of especially vulnerable patients.

To protect the privacy of patients, there should be an entrance separate from the rest of the hospital.

There should be a secure outdoor space.

Patients should have private rooms.

I would add that psychiatric wards should be aesthetically pleasing and comfortably furnished.

None of the hospitals in which I have been a patient could meet one of these standards. That is, I believe, because the primary consideration in the design of our psychiatric wards has been protection from legal liabilities rather than concern for the therapeutic needs of patients.

The Hospital 7

Incarceration in a psychiatric hospital feels like punishment. And, in an important way, it is punishment. The psychiatric hospital is, like the jail, a way of isolating from society people whose behavior disturbs the general order. Mad people disturb us in the same way that criminals do. They make us insecure. We feel safer knowing that they are locked up. The only difference is that criminals are locked up because they have been bad, while mad people are locked up (we say) for their own good. The canvas straightjacket, the leather bed restraints, the chemical sedatives have always been represented as symbols of benevolence. But they feel no more benevolent to the person bound in them than an iron cell door.

There is, however, one significant difference between the treatment of criminality and the treatment of madness. Criminals get fixed sentences. Madmen are sentenced for life. A man I know threw a chair at the judge who had just committed him to a psychiatric hospital. Thirty years later, he is still not free. Until the day he dies, because of that one moment of uncontrolled anger, he will be Mentally Ill and Dangerous. If you beat your baby to death, you can do your time and return to the world a free man. But for madmen, there is no atonement.

The Hospital 8

The arrangements of a psychiatric ward, so far as the patient is concerned, are immutable. Nothing can be moved or rearranged, nothing added, nothing subtracted, nothing hidden. There are no means to decorate a bedroom on a psychiatric ward. You cannot alter its appearance with a rug or a plant, change its color, hang a picture on the wall. Privacy is impossible. There is no way to fashion a place of refuge. The food is nondescript; it comes without condiments. The pocket-less clothes are hospital issue; there is no way to express an individual personality in the wearing of them. The schedule is fixed; the single way to rebel against it is to remain awake at night, but this sort of rebellion can and will be chemically quelled. The slightest impulses are subject to the rules; if you think you might like a cup of coffee or a piece of gum at 8:25, you'll have to wait; such requests can be fulfilled only on the hour. Any expression of personality beyond abject submission is likely to be regarded as a symptom of your illness and will, therefore, extend your incarceration.

A kind of society emerges in prisons. Prisoners develop their own rules and castes, form alliances, learn to speak a language peculiar to prisons, create their own underground economies, and are united by a common enemy, the staff. Their terms of stay are fixed. On the short-term psychiatric ward, none of these social possibilities is available. The length of your stay is indeterminate, and the requirements for release are largely, from your point of view, inscrutable. The way to freedom lies in assuming a false identity, that of a "patient." The word "patient" in itself is instructive. You learn to stop your tongue, to stifle your emotions, to question nothing, to practice obedience, to bide your time, patiently.

When you enter a psychiatric ward, you relinquish your possessions, your clothing, your freedom. You begin the process of earning your way back into the world. And to do that you must give up one more thing: the notion that you are an individual. You offer yourself, naked, as an object.

A Modest Proposal

Before admission to practice, every psychiatrist and psychiatric nurse should experience first-hand the kind of treatment they are going to give their patients. Each of them should be admitted anonymously to a psychiatric ward where they are not known. Each should arrive with a particularly pejorative diagnosis, paranoid schizophrenia, say, or Borderline Personality Disorder. Each should be appropriately medicated. Applicants will have two weeks to convince the staff, without reference to their credentials, that they are sane.

Those who fail will be allowed to try again in six months.

Bad Patients

I was on a psychiatric ward with an elderly woman, scarcely eighty pounds, who was getting around on a walker after a recent hip injury. She was a remarkably lively and intelligent woman with whom I had many wonderful conversations. But she was deeply troubled by two things. She was angry at her daughter, who had arranged for her hospitalization and then successfully advocated for her commitment. And she was anguished that she had been taken from her home without notice and was about to be sent to a distant city for some months with her affairs in disarray. Could she not, she repeatedly requested, be allowed two hours, even one hour, in her own home to gather her papers so that she could make a timely filing of her taxes, turn her furnace on, and see for herself that her house and possessions would be secure in her absence?

No, she could not, she was repeatedly told, it would violate policy to allow a patient to leave the ward before discharge. She could ask her daughter to do these things.

"But I don't trust my daughter and I don't want her in my house," the woman repeatedly replied. "I am not trying to escape," she said. "I will go and return in the company of the police or of as many phalanxes of social workers as you deem necessary. I simply need, for my own peace of mind, to see that my affairs are in order."

Her pleas, which would have broken the heart of anyone not a twenty-something social worker, fell on deaf ears. After a couple of weeks of this, the woman became somewhat belligerent. She was prescribed benzodiazepines to control her outbursts. These made her so incoherent that it almost seemed, at times, that her commitment to a locked nursing home for persons in advanced stages of dementia was justified.

On the day of her transfer, one of the burly six-foot sheriff's deputies went to the woman's room to secure her in handcuffs and leg chains for the ride. The other stood, not ten feet from me, in the patient day room with the social worker.

"That woman is a human being, you know," I said to the deputy. The social worker scowled but said nothing.

"Yes, I know," the deputy said.

"No you don't. If you did, you wouldn't treat her that way," I said.

The deputy hesitated for a long minute. Then he went to the woman's room and called out his partner. "I think we can leave the chains off," he said. "She's not going to run." He returned to the dayroom. In the awkward silence one could hear the soft bleat of the woman being presented with the handcuffs. "Oh, not really," she said. "I've never . . ."

"Well, you're going to have quite the ride today," the social worker suddenly said brightly.

"Difficult woman?"

"Difficult isn't the half of it. She is absolutely impossible. She whines, she complains, she yells, she throws things, she gets an idea into her head and heaven and earth cannot get it out of her. She demands special privileges, thinks, apparently, that she is some kind of queen. Obnoxious is the word. She is downright obnoxious. You'll get an earful today!" The two shared a pleasant laugh.

When the woman and her guards had left, I approached the social worker. "I think it was inappropriate of you to talk about a patient that way in front of me," I said.

"I'm sorry if I hurt your feelings."

"The issue is not my feelings. It's your behavior."

"I'm sorry if I hurt your feelings."

"Do you understand," I asked, "how a patient might imagine, over-hearing you, that you'd say similar things about him?"

"If you need help processing your emotions, I can arrange for you to see a counselor," she said.

She may have been the only person in that place who clearly knew the difference between a patient and a professional and the proper role of each.

Tremors 1

There were a dozen of us, all adults, sitting on kindergarten chairs around a table designed for toddlers. Each of us had been supplied with a pair of the blunt-nosed scissors familiar to preschoolers, a large blank card with holes punched in the upper corners, and a length of brightly colored yarn. At the center of the table were stacks of old women's magazines, pots of glue, and boxes of coloring crayons.

Our "therapist," the youngest person in the room, introduced the session. "Today we are going to make self-affirmation cards," she said. "Can anybody tell me what a self-affirmation is?"

I was a middle-aged college professor, the author of several books, the father of two grown children. I was damned if I was going to respond. Neither was anyone else. We all stared at her sullenly.

"Well," the young woman said, "a self-affirmation is something you like about yourself. Okay?" She put on a bright, stupid grin and looked around at us expectantly. We glared back.

"So who has an example? What is something you like about yourself?"

Silence. A person who is depressed enough to be hospitalized doesn't like anything about himself.

"Glenda, can you tell us something you like about yourself?"

Glenda looked blankly at the floor.

"Well, one thing I like about *myself* is that I am really good at organizing things. I like everything to be neat and tidy. That's a *self-affirmation*. That's something I like about myself. Okay?"

"Okay," a couple of people muttered.

"*Good*! I can see that we are getting the idea! Now Glenda, can you think of a self-affirmation for yourself? Something you like about yourself?"

Silence.

"I know this can be a hard idea to get, but I'm sure we all have something about ourselves that we like."

"I like that I'm not you, you fucking bastard," I thought.

"Hair," Glenda said. She managed both to spit the word out and to muffle it.

"Good, Glenda! You like your hair! And you do have lovely hair, Glenda. I can see why you're proud of it. I wish I had your hair. Mine will never stay where I want it to stay." She giggled. "So we all get the idea, right?"

Two or three nods.

"*Good*! Now here's what we're going to do," she said, although she herself intended to do nothing of the kind. "We are going to look through the magazines I have brought and find things—they could be pictures, they could be words—anything that reminds us of the things we like about ourselves. We are going to cut them out and paste them on these cards." She held one up. "You see that I have put the holes at the top. That's where the yarn will go. When we are finished, we will all have nice necklaces to wear that will remind us that we all have many wonderful points. Okay?"

There was a general lack of motion.

"We can all get started now. Okay?"

Silence.

"Any questions?"

Silence.

"*Great*! Then let's all get started! Okay?"

I stared at the table. I was trying to believe that my life had really come to this.

"How are we doing, Paul? Do we need some help?"

I shook my head, then instantly regretted it. I had been tricked into responding after all. My depression, which had been abating, was swelling up again. I forced my hand, which seemed like a thing separate from my body, to reach out and pick up the nearest magazine. The first thing I saw was an ad for Huggies diapers. I cut out the picture of a baby wearing one. "I'll say that I like it that I don't pee in my pants anymore," I thought. For an instant, I felt slightly better. And then the indignation welling up in me suddenly burst out. My hands began to shake violently. There was nothing I could do about it. I simply could not make my scissors work.

At the end of the session I was directed to an adjacent room. Two medical interns were waiting for me, their drug reference manuals in hand. They understood, one of them said, that I was experiencing tremors. I was induced to display my hands, which were still shaking. The interns asked a few questions, consulted their books, and prescribed a beta blocker. That, they said, should take care of my problem.

Six years later, I was taking my medications one morning when I noticed the little atenolol capsule in my hand. "Why am I taking that?" I wondered, and then I remembered. At last, something useful came out of that therapy session. I laughed a good long belly laugh. I could hardly wait to tell my psychiatrist why I thought one of my drugs could probably be safely discontinued.

Tremors 2

I have been looking at *Seeing the Insane,* in a fascinating study by Sander L. Gilman of images of the insane produced from the Fifteenth through the Nineteenth centuries. One finds the usual horrors. There are, for example, a couple of portraits of William Norris. Norris was an American sailor confined at England's Bethlem Asylum (from which derives the word *bedlam*). His existence was discovered by an outraged Member of Parliament, who arranged for his portrait to be drawn. Norris had been tethered, like a dog, to a chain, so that he could be yanked about at will by his keeper. He rebelled by packing the chain with straw so that it couldn't be retracted through the hole in his cell wall that accommodated it.

So he was fitted instead with an iron harness, riveted into place, which impaled his arms at his sides. The harness was attached to a twelve-inch chain that slid up and down a pole at his back. He was also chained by the legs. The result was that he could, with some effort, manage to sit up on his bench and to lie down, in one position only, on his back. He could not move his arms, he could not lean forward or backward, he could not stand up. When Norris was discovered, he had been confined in this manner for twelve years. The pictures of him reached the popular press and a sufficient uproar ensued so that major reforms were forced at the asylum. The great mystery, however, remains: Nobody with the right to call himself human would treat an animal in this way. How does it happen repeatedly that people in positions of absolute power treat their own fellows so brutally?

There are the usual absurdities, too. There are, for example, the portraits of those said to be mad by reason of masturbation, envy, vanity, religious fervor, gambling. There are the charts of a doctor who claimed to be able to diagnose imbecility on the basis of a single-line profile of patients' heads.

But what is most striking about the pictures Gilman presents is their remarkable continuity, down to the present day. Before I picked up Gilman's volume, I had been watching films depicting mental illness over the last thirty years. Many of these films are wholly sympathetic to their disturbed heroes or heroines, seeing them as fragile but worthy and even noble human beings. They are love stories, stories of triumph over adversity, stories of the wisdom to be found in unexpected places, and many of them are very moving. But from *One Flew Over the Cuckoo's Nest* right down to *Girl, Interrupted,* there is one jarring disjunct from reality, and it is straight out of the Fifteenth Century depictions of insanity. Every time a beautiful or handsome, sympathetic character with mental illness enters a psychiatric hospital, the scene becomes populated by freaks. The fellow inmates are invariably ugly. They pose in grotesque positions. They speak in imbecilic voices. When they sing, they are off-key. When they dance, they shuffle. When they laugh, they cackle. They are given to wild flights of manic misbehavior. They simper like babies. They huddle in fetal positions in the corners. The hero or heroine continues, however, to be recognizably human, freakish in context only for his or her continuing connection to normalcy.

The first time I woke up in a psychiatric ward, I ventured into the hallway with great trepidation. I expected to find what centuries of popular culture (and a good deal of medical culture as well) had prepared me to expect, a circus of freaks. Even before I stepped through the doorway, I was becoming enraged. I was not one of *those* people. But what I found was a group of patients who looked and acted quite normal. If you had given us proper clothes and distributed us among the weekend shoppers in the local mall, it would have been difficult to pick us out as the ones who were defective. This is a revelation so astonishing that it took two or three hospitalizations for me to realize that my first experience had not been an aberration. I had to get rid of the belief, which runs very deep, that insane people invariably *look* insane.

I was naturally interested, as I examined Gilman's study, to see how melancholia, the category of my own afflictions, had been represented. In early depictions, we carry bifurcated sticks, the origins of which are unclear, Gilman says. Sometimes this stick becomes a child's pinwheel, ridden, perhaps, as a hobbyhorse; hence its connection to fools, and to an infantile state of mind. It is also connected to the daemonic: the first published illustration of witches flying these sticks (later to become broomsticks) appeared in 1489. In other respects, representations of melancholia are unremarkable: they include the slumped posture, the downcast head, the haggard eyes, the frown at the mouth, the disheveled hair and clothes, all the things we would say make the very picture of depression.

Except, of course, that depression can't really be pictured. I once gave a speech, got a standing ovation, and was in my hotel room twenty minutes later, wondering how to kill myself. I doubt that anyone in my audience recognized that I was so severely depressed that I ought to have been under lock and key. I was able to function in public, of course, because it was not me but a person of the same name, an author, who gave the speech, and the author was not depressed.

The one remarkable feature in depictions of melancholia, constant through the centuries, is that its victims are almost always represented without hands. Either their hands are missing, or they are covered. The meaning here is probably obvious. A person without hands is helpless, defenseless, ineffectual, as dependent as an infant. And there are certainly many ways in which that is the effect of melancholia.

Modern medicine has brought new meaning to this image of depression. One of the adverse effects of a number of psychotropic medications is hand tremors. These can be severe enough to frustrate many simple acts, buttoning a shirt, for example, or writing with a pen, or drinking from a full glass. There have been many times when my hands trembled so violently that it was difficult to eat and I thought that I was going to have to resort to wearing a bib. Such disability is rare, to be sure, but fine hand tremors are not. They may be quite unnoticeable to others, but they make the patient who suffers from them self-conscious. One associates trembling hands, after all, with fear, nervousness, senility. So we curl our hands, we hide them in our laps, tuck them under tables, withdraw them into coat sleeves. We walk right back into the ancient pictures of melancholia.

Van Gogh

One notable exception in the history of artistic representations of insanity lies in the work of Vincent van Gogh. There are two portraits in van Gogh's oeuvre that bear uncanny similarities, one of them painted in 1889, the other in 1890. Both of the subjects sit at the same angle. They have the same nose, the same eyes, the same chin, the same moustache, the same wing-like tufts of side hair. Their clothes drape in the same manner. They are rendered in similar colors. They have the same doleful and somewhat weary expression. They both exude the same air of intensity. If one knew nothing about these paintings, one would say that they are alternative views of the same man, or portraits of brothers. In fact, however, one is a painting of a hospital patient, and the other is a portrait of the psychiatrist with whom van Gogh spent his last days. And there is one difference: Dr. Gachet is portrayed with hands; the insane man isn't.

Van Gogh himself, of course, was a patient in insane asylums and killed himself at the age of 37. Does his inability to see the difference between one of his fellow inmates and one of his doctors mean that the difference was not visible? Or does it only mean that it takes a sane man to see the difference?

Going to Electroconvulsive Therapy (ECT)

It is 6:30 in the morning. You dress in a hospital gown, robe, and paper booties. You remove your dentures, watch, and glasses. Someone comes with a wheelchair to take you upstairs. Entering a hospital means giving up the right to walk. A row of gurneys is lined up in the hallway outside the surgery room. You take off your robe, climb onto one of the gurneys, and lie down. The side rails are raised. An attendant covers you in a warmed blanket. A nurse inserts an IV needle into one of the veins in your left hand. You feel a sharp, scraping pain. By the end of the week, she will have to switch to your right hand and find a vein that is useable. You wait. The pediatric surgery must be nearby because babies in tall cribs roll rapidly past you, in and out of the recovery room. The babies are hooked up to IV bottles. They are crying. The hallway is full of the odor of sweet chemicals. They make you feel sick.

Someone is wheeled out of the surgery room, and someone else is wheeled in. Your gurney is advanced one space in the line. The doctor, the nurse, the anesthesiologist, talk about their weekends, what kind of new car to buy, the state of the stock market, anything but what they are doing. The metallic buzz of the ECT machine sounds. You wince. Another person is wheeled out and another one in. You advance one more space in the line. You close your eyes and try to relax. Another buzz, another gurney comes out of the surgery.

You go in head first. It is a tiny room, barely enough space for the gurney and the three staff members. No matter how many times you have done this, you are afraid. Your gown is pulled down and EKG monitors are pasted onto your chest. A blood pressure cuff is attached to your arm and inflated. The anesthesiologist inserts a needle into your IV and pushes the plunger. You feel the cold chemicals crawling up your arm. Very soon they will paralyze you and render you unconscious. (In the days when the procedure was still known as electroshock, neither of these niceties was observed.

Patients sometimes broke their backs in the violence of the convulsions.) An oxygen mask is placed over your nose. You recognize its sweet, nauseating smell.

In a second or two, everything goes blank.

Getting ECT

Two dabs of a conducting gel are smeared on your head. This is where the two electrodes will be placed. Ugo Cerletti, who invented the procedure, first tried it out on dogs. He placed one electrode in the dog's mouth and the other in the anus. But half of the dogs died. Then he heard of a slaughtering house in town that electrocuted pigs. He went there and observed how this was done. An electrical current was applied to their heads, and then the pigs' throats were cut. They didn't die from the shock but from the bleeding! Cerletti confirmed this with his own experiments on pigs. It was time to try the procedure on a human.

An incoherent man who had been referred to Cerletti's clinic by police was chosen. He was given an electrical charge to the head. It seemed to make no difference in his behavior. Dr. Cerletti tried the procedure a second time, at a higher voltage. Still no change. But when Cerletti prepared to make a third try, at a higher voltage still, the patient cried, "Stop! You'll kill me." There was no patient consent in Italy in those Fascist days. The man was given another shock. He recovered from it and sat up. He spoke in coherent sentences. That is how the procedure you are about to submit to was born.

The electrodes are applied to your head. You are given a zap of electricity. A firestorm goes off in your head. The brain convulses. Your hand, the one part of you that has not been paralyzed, twitches. The seizure lasts anywhere from thirty seconds to a minute. When it is finished, you are unhooked from the measuring devices and taken to a recovery room. You will awaken in fifteen or twenty minutes.

Waking up After ECT

Your eyes open. You try to think where you are, but can't remember. There is sunlight, you can see that. You are surprised. For some reason, you would have thought it would be dark. You can see that you are lying in a hospital bed. Your arm is attached to a blood pressure cuff. You know what the cuff is for, but you can't remember what it's called. Has your heart given out? Have you had surgery? There don't seem to be any bandages, except a small one on your right hand. Your heart seems to be working. Have you been in an accident? Perhaps your injuries are internal. Perhaps there was nothing they could do for you, and they have sent you here to die. That must be it. You are dying. But why have they told no one? Why are you here alone? You are suddenly afraid. Am I prepared to die? you ask yourself, but you don't remember how to think about such a question. You close your eyes. A vague thought crosses your mind: Weren't you in some other kind of hospital recently? Perhaps a psychiatric ward? You look around again. No, this is not a psychiatric ward. The bed is comfortable. There is wallpaper on the walls, and some kind of picture. Didn't you used to wear glasses? You can't remember. There is a television set, a telephone. It is quiet. Thank God for that. It seems that you have been longing for a little quiet, but you can't think why. Even in the quietness, your head throbs. The sunlight coming through the window is piercing. Perhaps you have had a brain injury. Have you become a zombie? It could be. You see yourself in a bib being spoon-fed mashed banana.

Someone comes with a wheelchair and takes you away. An elevator door opens. You clearly recognize it as a psychiatric ward. But why are they taking you here? This isn't a proper place for dying. You are put to bed. You feel more tired than you have ever felt in your life. But you also have to pee. You find the bathroom. While you are standing at the toilet, everything dissolves into a swirl. The next thing you know, you are lying in the shower stall. A nurse towers above you. You follow his gaze. You have wet your pajamas. You want to cry, like a little boy.

Baby 1

I know, I know. It is a very small thing, and there are much bigger matters to fret about, even in hospital psychiatric wards. But it has always bothered me that I have been issued Johnson's baby shampoo when I have been a psychiatric patient. I don't like going around smelling like a baby. It is a painful reminder of the infantile status to which I have descended. There are a great many plush toys on psychiatric wards. The movies that are sometimes shown on weekends are always appropriate for viewing by small children. A lot of coloring goes on. Once, a man on the ward brought Thomas the Tank bed sheets to replace the hospital ones. In many ways, a psychiatric ward is like a day care center, except that Mommy doesn't come to pick you up at the end of the day.

Baby 2

In many ways, as I have suggested, psychiatric hospitals treat their patients as infants. In doing so, they teach them that the way to wellness lies in being infantile. For example:

If you are bedridden, it is customary to wear pajamas. Otherwise, healthy adults and children alike, in our culture, wear street clothes during the day and bedclothes at night. The exception is infants, who wear "sleepers" all the time. In my experience mental health patients who, although they are ambulatory, are required to wear pajamas all day, whatever the reasons for this policy, are being given the explicit message that they are like infants.

The only people who do not customarily wear shoes when they are up and about are babies and mental patients.

An adult in socks and pajamas who is being interviewed by a psychiatrist wearing a suit and tie is explicitly put in the position of playing the child to the adult.

Plastic-covered mattresses and pillows are no doubt there for hygienic reasons, but the message that is conveyed is, "We anticipate that you will, like a baby, wet yourself."

If you have to go elsewhere in the hospital for medical treatment, you are required, even though you are perfectly ambulatory, to get there in a wheelchair, just as babies, when they go out, travel in strollers.

Bathrooms on psychiatric wards are carefully designed to be hazard free. Shower curtain rods are designed to collapse when weight is put on them. There are no surfaces to which you might attach a bed sheet. There are no interior locks; you can't barricade yourself in such a bathroom. Nothing is breakable. The only conceivable hazard in a bathroom on a psychiatric ward is that you might try to drown yourself in the toilet bowl. Although that is not inconceivable, the chances of success are highly unlikely. Still, if you are suicidal, your bathroom door will be locked, and you will be required, like a small child, to ask permission to use it.

The evening meal is served not at an hour when adults customarily eat but at five p.m., the children's hour.

The only diversion customarily offered is "occupational therapy," which consists almost entirely of nursery school activities.

Nurses on psychiatric wards, except in the exceptional case of a patient who also has a serious physical illness, interact with patients by taking their vital signs and delivering meals and medications. Otherwise, their chief function, so far as patients are concerned, is as babysitters.

On many acute care wards, the only things a patient can do by himself are to take care of his personal hygiene and to feed himself. In all other respects, he is rendered as helpless as a toddler.

There are undoubtedly good reasons for existing policies. I do not wish to suggest that they are entirely arbitrary and capricious. But quite aside from their practicalities, they carry a powerful symbolism: You are not a responsible adult; you are nothing but a baby.

It is not clear to me how this message promotes emotional healing.

Baby 3

To assume sickness as a career, of course, is to resume the role of a child. As Thomas Szasz has pointed out, children are largely defined by what they cannot or are not allowed to do. Once I had become professionally ill, I was no longer able to work, to manage my own affairs without the supervision of a social worker, to be trusted with my own medications, to represent myself in court. I was officially classified as a "vulnerable adult," as someone, that is, who requires the same legal protections as a child.

On the occasions when I was hospitalized, it was judged that I was not even competent to be left alone. I needed, like an infant, to be watched twenty-four hours a day. As a baby is kept in a playpen, I was kept in a locked ward. In fact, except for social convention there is no reason why mental patients should not be diapered, dressed in sleepers, and bottle-fed. This might even be therapeutic. It might shock patients into realizing their actual standing.

This idea has, in fact, been tentatively explored. Prisoners in solitary confinement have been fed baby food. Adults in halfway houses have been kept in symbolic diapers until they earn their way to higher status. And mentally ill adults, who are otherwise capable, are regularly sent to "foster homes." It was once suggested, by a therapist, that I should be placed in one. This was a rare moment in my parenting by the mental health system when I felt genuinely alarmed. It is an odd experience to hear adults speaking about their foster moms and dads, meaning not those who raised them but the people with whom they are currently living. When they do, they sound just like children. They talk about the way in which their "parents" are becoming mean or unfair. They speak of their resentments against their "siblings," that is, the other adults being cared for in the same place. They brag about the things their "moms" bought them yesterday or the places their "dads" took them. I know one such foster "child" who doesn't have a key to the house she lives in. Since she is always being watched, she doesn't need one.

The reward in resuming the role of a child is that you get to live a child's responsibility-free life. You have to accept the sometimes annoying rules of childhood, it is true, but play becomes, on the other hand, the sole work of your life. I re-entered childhood because I felt like an abysmal failure. I didn't want to expect anything of myself anymore. The only success expected of a child, as the New Age phrase now popular among therapists has it, is to "be in the moment." As an officially sanctioned man-child, I wasn't even expected to grow up.

Baby 4

Now we put all our babies in diapers and feed them from bottles and let them sleep as much as they like. When they are hungry they cry; both Elizabeth and Erik had trouble learning to do that. When they are older they chew on teething rings and pretzels and start eating traditional baby foods. Eventually they learn to crawl, to talk, and begin to feed themselves. The two-year-old negativist stage is always a problem. For a while I thought Eric might never get toilet trained.

JACQUI LEE SCHIFF

The "babies" Schiff is referring to are all adults with schizophrenia. Her "re-parenting therapy" was developed in the late 1960s and early 1970s. At the time, the theory that mental illnesses are caused by bad parenting was still popular. Schiff took the theory to its logical and literal extreme. If bad parenting is the cause of schizophrenia, she reasoned, then the best way to cure it is to start people over by turning them into infants again and raising them with new and more satisfactory parents. She claimed great results. This is not surprising. Every kind of therapy—and there is no therapy so weird that it has not been tried by somebody—claims a success rate of seventy to eighty percent, on the basis of "scientific" studies.

Schiff's idea of ideal parenting included beating patients. Spankings were an important element in her method, and she emphasized that the spankings needed to be hard enough to inflict serious pain. She was eventually forced to abandon her treatments when one of her "babies" was scalded to death in a bathtub, but she did not, like ordinary murderers, go to jail. Indeed, she soon resurfaced on the lecture circuit, and there are, to this day, professional advocates of her methods.

It is one measure of the agony of schizophrenia that sufferers could be found to submit to this debasement, and that there were real parents

112

who were willing to sanction it. And it is a measure of the power of psychotherapists in our society that Schiff could publish a book frankly describing her methods, that it could become a best-seller, and that, when the book appeared, she was neither laughed nor shamed out of business.

A Brief History
of Modern Psychiatric Treatments

Late Eighteenth Century

The Bath of Surprise: The patient was led blindfolded across a room to a trapdoor, which plunged him into a tub of cold water. The fright was the therapeutic element.

Simulated drowning: The patient was thrown into the sea and his head was held down until he was nearly dead. Or he was locked into a box with holes drilled into it or into an iron cage and submerged in a pond until the desired state of near-death was achieved.

The Swinging Chair: The patient was secured in a swinging chair which was then swirled until he vomited, had convulsions, or soiled himself, and showed signs of acute exhaustion.

Nausea: Mercury and other chemicals were used to induce intense and prolonged nausea.

Vomiting: Various vomit-inducing agents were used to make patients violently ill.

Caustics: The patient's head was shaved and caustics were spread on it, producing excruciating sores, which the patient might, in his agony, spread to his genitals and other parts of his body, multiplying the beneficial effect. This, it is worth noting, is one of the tortures that Satan visited upon Job.

Beating.

Malnourishment.

114 | The Tranquilizer Chair: A device into which the nude patient was strapped in a sitting position, the extremities bound, the head immobilized by a wooden device that also obscured vision. There was a hole in the seat and a bucket beneath for elimination. After days, or

even in some cases, hours, in this contraption, patients were said to become remarkably docile.

Nineteenth Century

Moral therapy: Patients were housed in small numbers in countryside asylums of architectural distinction where there were flowerbeds and gardens, tended by those who lived there. Superintendents were expected to be mild in manner, humane in outlook, and knowledgeable about all of their patients; they took their meals with them. Patients were treated, to the fullest extent possible, as rational. They lived in semi-private, well-furnished and decorated rooms. The restraints were used only as a last resort. There were libraries, theatrical performances, evening lectures, sporting events, and other diversions to keep patients' minds occupied. Physical exercise was part of the routine. Staff members identified themselves as companions.

Twentieth Century

Hydrotherapy: Patients were tightly bound like mummies in wet sheets so that they could move only their fingers, toes, and necks. Then they were strapped to their beds. They lay there, in their own accumulating wastes, while the sheets dried. As they did, the sheets tightened, and the temperature rose inside them, so that the experience was like being trapped in a burning vise.

Refrigeration therapy: Patients were wrapped in refrigerated blankets, their body temperatures were lowered by ten to twenty degrees Fahrenheit, and they were kept in this state for up to three days. Or they were put into refrigerated cabinets, packed with ice, and kept there for a day or two. The refrigeration was repeated as necessary. Unfortunately, too many patients died, and this treatment had to be abandoned.

Sterilization.

Extraction of the teeth.

Endocrine therapy: One popular extract was made from the thyroid glands of sheep. These extracts, when injected, made patients extremely ill, but it was said that when patients recovered they were also better mentally.

Deep-sleep therapy: Barbiturates were used to keep patients asleep, sometimes for weeks at a time.

Fever therapy: Patients were given malaria.

Insulin therapy: Patients were given insulin until they lapsed into coma and then they were revived with a sugar solution.

Metrazol therapy: A synthetic preparation of camphor was used to induce seizures.

Electroshock therapy: An electrical current is used to induce seizures.

Prefrontal lobotomy: The patient was given a local anesthetic. A hammer was used to tap ice picks into the skull above the eyes. The picks were then pulled upwards, destroying tissue in the frontal lobes of the brain.

Drug therapy: Came of age in the 1970s. Thorazine, form of a drug that had been previously used as an insecticide and a pig-dewormer, was the first important modern psychotropic medication. All psychotropic drugs have adverse effects. Some of them compromise long-term health: weight gain, liver damage, adult-onset diabetes, and changes in blood pressure, for example. Some of them, whatever their benefits, make life significantly less pleasurable: hand tremors, facial tics, drowsiness, lethargy, anxiety, impotence, incontinence, for example. And a few of the adverse effects are potentially fatal. Unless you had reason to believe that they might be helpful, you would not want to take them.

Quiz

Question: Which of the treatments previously cited was not introduced by scientists?

Answer: Moral therapy. It was developed by the Quakers.

Treatments

The lobotomies of the 1940s and 1950s were among the crudest and most destructive surgeries of the twentieth century. The man who developed the procedure, Antonio Egas Moniz, won a Nobel Prize in Medicine in 1949 for his work.

Medications 1

There are people who think that medications are poisons, and others who see them as a psychiatric conspiracy, and others—mostly people who have not suffered from mental illness, I believe—who bemoan the arrival of the Prozac Generation. Nobody I know enjoys taking medications. I, like many others who are mentally ill, have tried on a number of occasions to quit them, always with disastrous results. But I have never felt entirely well on them either, and I have heard others say the same. I think I know why. Just as pain medication masks the pain, but does nothing to correct its source, so psychotropic medications bring relief from psychic pain without changing its underlying causes. Psychotropic medications are not treatments for mental illness. They are palliatives.

The only known way to cure the psyche is for the individual himself to effect its repair. That is a long, lonely, miserable, and exceedingly complicated undertaking, not least because it requires dismantling the defenses that have allowed the anguished repairman to survive in the first place. What does one do in the interval while one is defenseless? It might be the role of hospitals to provide a secure and nurturing place during this time of exposure. But that would require, for one thing, that hospitals were kind to the soul, which they are not. And it would require time. But insurance companies have expediently bought the argument that mental illnesses are strictly brain diseases, treatable by medication. They are no longer willing to pay for the time it would take to bring about authentic healing. Time and safety, alas, have become the two rarest commodities in the modern world.

Medications 2

The popular belief persists that antidepressant medications make people happy. They don't. When they work, they make people not-depressed. But there is as wide a gulf between being not-depressed and being happy as there is between being not-starving and well nourished, or not-mute and eloquent. One speaks to the condition of living and the other to its art. What we are is far more important than what we are not.

To realize that our knowledge is ignorance,

This is a noble insight.

To regard our ignorance as knowledge,

This is mental sickness.

LAO TZU

Understanding

I have yet to meet a therapist who took to heart C. G. Jung's advice: "Nothing is more unbearable for the patient than to be always understood."

Change 1

I used to give my humanities students the hopelessly difficult problem of devising a test for normalcy. Nobody, of course, could ever succeed at this task; there was always excellent reason for rejecting as too narrow every standard that was proposed. But the astonishing fact is that mental health professionals not only think they know when human behavior is abnormal—a claim that presupposes the ability to define normalcy—but they imagine that they have devised, in the diagnostic criteria of the *Diagnostic and Statistical Manual* (the *DSM*), an at least quasi-scientific standard for identifying and differentiating it.

I lost, in the space of eighteen months, my wife of thirty-three years, my health (physical and emotional), my work (teaching), my vocation (writing), my financial independence, my home, my dogs, my library, my piano, and contact with my children. I only narrowly escaped with my life, which I did not want and tried to take. When I failed to respond to the usual elixirs—mood stabilizers, anti-depressants, tranquilizers, anti-psychotics, and electroconvulsive therapy—prescribed by a psychiatrist who could only see me for a few minutes every few months, the powers that be consulted the DSM and concluded that I was suffering from a personality disorder. The problem with my mood lay, in other words, not in the catastrophe of my life, but in certain pathological defects of my character.

Life's circumstances cannot be changed, but character defects can be, or so the therapists hope. I was enrolled in something called Dialectical Behavioral Therapy, which is the last word in the treatment of people, mainly women, who are thought to have the personality flaws associated with Borderline Personality Disorder. I was assigned to a therapist who specializes in the disorder. So began my year-long, twice-weekly immersion in the business of personality adjustment. I say business because this service cost ten thousand dollars.

Abandonment 1

A friend writes, "What would happen if you replaced, "I lost, within the space of eighteen months . . ." with, "I abandoned, within the space of eighteen months, my wife . . .'?" A reasonable question. I replied:

Did I abandon my marriage? Yes. Twice, once emotionally and a second time when I attempted suicide. Was this a solitary act for which I should bear sole responsibility? I don't know, but I don't think so. My guess is that we had both abandoned the marriage long before it was formally ended, and that our relationship was mutually poisonous.

Did I abandon my physical health? To the extent that I did not take good care of myself while I was depressed, yes, I was responsible for my diabetes and my heart problems. It is also true, however, that both depression and the medications I was taking for it may have been complicating factors. Depression has been linked to both diabetes and heart disease, Seroquel has been linked to diabetes, and Effexor causes high blood pressure.

Did I abandon my emotional health? After a long period of neglect, I tried to face up to it. I tried hospitalization, partial hospitalization, several kinds of medication, and three kinds of talk therapy. To the extent that these failed, I may have been responsible for sabotaging them. That is, at any rate, what my last therapist thought I had done.

Did I abandon teaching? I quit my full-time teaching position even though I was offered a $10,000-a-year raise to stay on, for two reasons: Because I could not handle both my depression and a full teaching load, and because my wife hated the town we were living in and emphatically did not want to stay there. I was then fired from the part-time teaching job I took in this manner: The dean of a new member college in our consortium came to a board meeting at which I was present. He said he was enthusiastic about the program but could not deliver students from his college unless one of his English teachers was hired to take over the writing courses. There was a silence. Then one of the board members said, "With due respect, Paul, I guess that's what we have to do." There was no discussion. The vote was unanimous. I do not believe I was the active agent in this transaction.

Did I abandon my writing? I proposed a new book, got a contract for it, and made a serious effort, over a period of two years, to produce it. But I was completely blocked. I couldn't write a single sentence of it, although I did do a lot of research. I entered weekly therapy to try to break the block, but I couldn't do it. So I returned the advance. Did I give up? Yes. Was this a reasonable thing to do? I don't know.

Did I abandon my financial independence? I applied for disability. In that sense, yes. But at the time, I saw no other choice. I was not employable, I was broke, and I had no access to our joint assets. The alternatives that had been spoken of were my placement in a foster home, or my admission to a state hospital for long-term therapy. I think I made the best of a bad set of choices.

Did I abandon my possessions? To the extent that I gave up my right to them when I attempted suicide, yes.

Did I abandon my children? After my suicide attempt, I kept in e-mail contact with one of my children, and I telephoned the other almost every day for two months and never made contact. To the extent that their distance was due to my bad parenting or to earlier abandonment on my part, yes. To the extent that I stopped attempting to contact one of my children, yes. My therapist suggested to me that I ought to do so, although, of course, I alone am responsible for my actions. Was I wrong to do what I did? I don't know. I love my children deeply and, no matter what, I always will.

To answer these questions in the affirmative requires, as I see it, two further assumptions: that my depression was, or ought reasonably to have been, within my control; and that my attempt at suicide was the act of a rational man who ought, in the moment, to have known better and who could have reasonably have been expected to take charge of himself. These assumptions suggest that I was not, in fact, ill, but was, rather, willfully and deliberatively self-destructive; that is, that I knew, at the time, that there were alternatives and refused to consider or take them.

Whether or not these events in my life were due to abandonment on my part, they entailed heavy losses, over which I felt deep grief. In the aftermath, which might have been the more helpful therapy? Should I have been encouraged to embrace and live through my grief and then guided toward an examination of the ways in which I had enabled my own destruction? Or should I have been told that my problem was that I was an abnormally flawed human being and set to work on learning a set of rules for fixing up my defective character? That's the question I was trying to raise. Perhaps it was the wrong question. It could be that in asking it, I was trying to deflect attention from my own culpabilities.

Abandonment 2

There is a place I could, but won't, go. I could inquire into the ways in which I have been abandoned, or have felt so. But that's the past. The past can be remembered. It can, faintly, be understood. But it cannot be revised or amended. Let it be. For the moment, the only important things are this room, this black chair, this desk, this piece of paper.

The Stoics were right. What happens, happens. It cannot hurt you. But what you think has happened, that is an altogether different, and potentially lethal, matter.

Diagnosis 1

I was shattered, as I think most psychiatric patients are, by the diagnosis that what was wrong with me was a defect of character, and that I had, furthermore, the worst possible kind of character flaw. Marsha Linehan, the leading scholar of Borderline Personality Disorder, has described the borderline patient as "someone in whom everything that can go wrong has gone wrong." With the possible exception of schizophrenia, no other diagnosis in psychiatry quite so efficiently shreds the last vestiges of selfhood. In the end, character is all we've got. "Character," Heraclites said a very long time ago, "is fate." It is what makes a person who he is. Everything else about us is ephemeral. Repeatedly during our lifetimes, every single cell in our bodies is replaced by new ones. The only thing about us that endures and makes us in any way unique, in any way identifiably human, is our character. How do you respond when a professional in such matters looks at you casually across a desk and says, "What's wrong with you is who you are"?

I was knocked flat, in the same way, by reading this entry in my therapist's notes: "Patient is still not leading a life worth living."

"That's not your decision to make," I said to myself when I read it.

And I maintain that position. Some of the language of modern psychiatry is as brutal and callous as were the physical tortures that the insane suffered in the eighteenth century. It masquerades as diagnostics, just as keeping the mentally ill chained in dungeons on beds of straw purported to be treatment. In fact, however, it is eviscerating judgmental. Words, despite the old saw about sticks and stones, can cut as deeply as the lash. I know. I have felt the wounds.

The Genealogy of a Diagnosis

1801: Mania without Delirium. The first formal suggestion that someone could be mentally ill without being deluded.

1835: Mania without Delirium begat Moral Insanity.

1881: Moral Insanity begat Psychopathic Personality.

1905: Psychopathic Personality begat The Moral Defective.

1941: The Moral Defective begat The Mask of Sanity.

About 1950: The Mask of Sanity begat Borderline Personality
Disorder. The idea was that people with this disorder were on the
borderline between neurosis and psychosis.

1994: Borderline Personality Disorder begat, in the *DSM-IV,* ten dis-
tinct kinds of personality disorder.

Mental illnesses, like families, grow over time. Today, there are more
ways to be mentally ill than any other time in history.

Diagnosis 2

In 1850, the Louisiana Medical Society established a commission to study "African Americans." One matter that concerned the commission was the tendency of some, but not all, slaves to run away from their masters. The explanation, the commission concluded, was that those who fled were suffering from drapetomania. They were, that is, insane.

Diagnosis 3

There is a certain amount of serendipity in who gets judged insane and who doesn't. The classic demonstration of this is a pair of experiments conducted in 1972 by the psychologist David L. Rosenhan.

In the first experiment, Rosenhan and seven volunteers presented themselves, under pseudonyms, at twelve different psychiatric hospitals. There were three women and five men. They included three psychologists, a pediatrician, a psychiatrist, a painter, a housewife, and a graduate student in psychology. All were completely sane and without any previous history of mental illness. The hospitals were located in five different states on the East and West coasts and varied widely in reputation, resources, and means of funding.

In each instance, the "patients" presented with an identical complaint. They said they were hearing voices, and that these were indistinct but seemed to say "empty," "hollow," and "thud." Males reported the voices as male, females reported them as female. The symptoms were chosen because they did not correspond to any diagnosis then in the psychiatric literature. Those in the psychiatric profession claimed other occupations, so that they would not trigger any special consideration on the part of the hospital staff. Otherwise, the "patients" told the truth about themselves and behaved in every way as they normally would.

All eight volunteers were duly admitted. Seven of them were diagnosed with schizophrenia and the eighth with bipolar disorder. They were started on medications, which the volunteers tongued, and held for observation. One of the "patients" was released in seven days, another was kept in the hospital for fifty-two days. The average length of stay was nineteen days. Eventually they were all released, but not as sane individuals. In each case, the release documents described them as persons with severe mental illnesses that were "in remission."

After the experiment was over, Rosenhan combed the hospital and nursing records for any indication that any of the medical or nursing staff had suspected that any one of the "patients" was actually well. No such evidence emerged. For the first three stays, however, an accurate count was kept of the reactions of the other patients. Nearly a third of them identified the volunteers as ringers.

Rosenhan then arranged for a second experiment at a research and teaching hospital. There, the staff was informed that within the next three months, one or more pseudopatients would seek to be admitted. Staff were asked to rate the likelihood that each new admission was a fake. During the three months, 193 patients were admitted to the hospital. Forty-one of those patients were identified as suspect, with high confidence, by at least one staff member. In twenty-three cases, at least one psychiatrist was strongly suspicious. And nineteen of the patients were regarded as highly suspect by both a psychiatrist and at least one other staff member. In fact, however, none of the patients was sent there by Rosenhan.

"We now know," Rosenhan concluded, "that we cannot distinguish insanity from sanity." And this, he said, is the problem: "A diagnosis of cancer that has been found to be in error is a cause for celebration. But psychiatric diagnoses are rarely found in error. The label sticks, a mark of inadequacy forever."

So far as I know, Rosenhan's experiments have not been repeated. But they need to be replicated, in as many guises as can be imagined, over and over again, either until psychiatric diagnosis can be built upon reliable science, or until a suitable humility attends the practice of diagnosis.

Diagnosis 4

I have been treated by six psychiatrists and by six psychologists. The psychiatrists have all believed that my problem was organic. The psychologists have all believed that my problem was behavioral. We see what we are trained to see.

Diagnosis 5

There are three ways to treat a mental illness like clinical depression. There are drugs, which are thought to alter brain chemistry. There is electroconvulsive therapy, which does something, presumably physical, although nobody knows quite what it is. These two options are "medical" options. They treat mental illness, that is, as an organic disorder, no different in kind than, say, heart disease or diabetes.

Then there is psychotherapy, which treats mental illness as a malfunctioning not of the body but of the self. What needs fixing, from the psychotherapist's point of view, is not some part of you, but who you fundamentally are. Some physical illnesses profoundly challenge one's sense of who one is—paralysis, for example. And some medical treatments do the same, for instance, radical mastectomy. But the underlying cause of the pathology—damaged nerves or cancer in these instances—is not *personal*. The illness or the treatment may require you to adjust your sense of who you are to new realities, the loss of some functions, perhaps, or changes in appearance. But they do not require you to believe that there was something wrong with who you were before the onset of illness, or that you yourself are the cause of your afflictions. You are quite obviously the victim of events largely beyond your control.

The psychotherapist, however, stands in relation to the patient not as a doctor but as a priest. "Sin" and "personality disorder" are different labels, but they carry the same substantive weight. Priest and psychotherapist alike exist to help you to see that your troubles, however understandably, perhaps even unavoidably, are of your own making. The priest and the psychotherapist both speak the language of rebirth. The way to salvation or to health, they both say, lies in becoming a new person.

In this shattering respect, mental illness is unlike any other kind of illness.

Carols for the Mentally Ill

Schizophrenia: Do You Hear What I Hear?

Multiple Personality Disorder: We Three Queens Disoriented Are

Dementia: I Think I'll Be Home for Christmas

Narcissism: Hark the Herald Angels Sing About Me

Mania: Deck the Halls and Walls and Houses and Lawns and Streets and Stores and Towns and Cars and Busses and Trucks and Trees and Fire Hydrants and . . .

Paranoia: Santa Clause is Coming to Get Me

Borderline Personality Disorder: I Dream of Roasting on an Open Fire

There are no facts, only interpretations.

Change 2

I was going to write about the year I spent getting my character adjusted in twice-a-week therapy sessions, but I realize now that the experience can adequately be summarized in a sentence or two. The therapy utterly failed because I never believed in it. And I did not believe in it because I knew that I was grieving half a dozen substantial losses, all of them unresolved. Any one of them might have explained my despair. I didn't need to be defective in character to be unhappy. But I did need to acknowledge my grief, to feel it, and to find a way through it. I didn't need somebody to explain me to myself, or fix me or teach me how to manage myself in six easy steps. I need somebody to *listen*. And because I didn't get that, I lost an entire year of my life.

An Alternative Explanation

It is true that my therapy failed because I didn't believe in it. It is also true that it failed because I didn't want it to succeed. Why would a suffering patient want therapy to fail? A person with a bodily complaint normally goes to a doctor to get relief. Why should a person who is mentally ill be any different?

I believe that my own descent into disability by reason of mental illness came about in four stages. First, I was given permission to use my illness as an excuse for idleness. Second, my life after "recovery" did not go well. Third, I tried to kill myself. Fourth, when I failed, the attempt became reason to launch myself upon a new career as a mental patient.

Illness as a reason for idleness. After the breakdown I had in my early forties, I saw a therapist who said to me, "Look, Paul, you've just been through a major trauma. You need time to recover. If you had just had open heart surgery, you wouldn't expect to get up in the morning and run a marathon. You would give yourself time to heal. Quit working for a while. Relax. Give yourself some breathing room." This, as it turned out, was exactly what I wanted to hear.

I took three months off. It was my first period of an extended idleness in thirty years. Until then, work had been my religion. I wrote a long essay on my honeymoon. When we vacationed I took a typewriter along and wrote every morning. The rest of the time I was bored and miserable. During my years as a newspaperman, I often worked seven days a week, twelve or fourteen hours a day, except on Sunday, when I went to church in the morning. On the side, I wrote a book and taught college classes. I believed that if I worked hard enough, I might be saved.

138

Those three months off were marvelous. I saw a movie almost every day. I spent hours a day listening to music. I took long walks with my dogs. I did volunteer work on a vegetable farm, physical labor of a kind I had last known as a teenager. I remembered how much I enjoyed it.

I got to know my children. Normally I would have felt guilty as hell about such a vacation, but now I could say that I was taking one on doctor's orders, for my health. I had a face-saving reason for not working. The medications I was taking for the first time confirmed my illness. And, in fact, I did begin to feel better. Before long, I felt well enough to resume work.

Adversity. Ten years later, my world collapsed again. In those years I wrote six books, taught full-time, attended more meetings of more committees than I could count, and gave a speech wherever two or three were gathered together. I used my work to hide from myself. In one especially frenetic period, I gave sixty speeches in five weeks. The early books were commercial failures but critical successes. Then came two books that didn't even get reviewed in the local papers. I quit two teaching jobs because I was too depressed to go on. I was fired from a third. A famous writer with whom I had once had a casual friendship launched a biting attack on my work. "My idea of death," he said at one point, "would be to be stuck in a cabin in the North Woods for two weeks with nothing to read but Paul Gruchow's books." I was mortified. My friends said to me, "Get over it, Paul. Who cares if somebody doesn't like your books? That's inevitable. It doesn't mean a thing." But I wouldn't get over it because I agreed with my critic. My books *were* crap. They were boring, trite, sanctimonious. I had not read any of them after they were published. I knew that if I did, I would not like what I found. For the next three years I was unable to write a word. Then my marriage, which had been faltering for years, began to collapse outright.

Suicide. I finally decided one night, when my wife was away at work, that death was the only way out. I gathered a soup bowl full of pills and, sitting at my desk, downed them with a bottle of whiskey. Just before I fell unconscious, however, I dialed 911.

Illness as a career. When I became aware of myself again, I was in the hospital, on a psychiatric ward. I was too miserable to mind. And, in a way, the ward was comforting. There were all the trappings of medicine, the taking of vital signs morning and night, the medications, the nurses and doctors who were plainly concerned about me. I could see what I had been denying, that my life mattered to somebody else.

I was transferred from the private hospital to a state institution, where it was anticipated that I would spend at least several weeks. After six days, I was discharged. I was furious. I threw two tantrums the day I was told I was leaving. I was not prepared to go back into the world again. It was suggested that I should apply for Social Security disability. Without a moment's hesitation, I did. Normally this is a long process involving a series of rejections and appeals. My application was approved without question in three weeks. This confirmed to me that I was indeed a very sick man.

Over the next year I was re-hospitalized five or six times. I grew to hate hospitals, but also to depend upon them. I underwent several series of ECT treatments, which I knew were reserved for the sickest patients. When I was out of the hospital, my time was occupied with various therapeutic appointments: visits to my doctors, consultations with my case manager, trips to the outreach nurse who dispensed my medications, therapy sessions. At some point, I stopped thinking of myself as a writer. I had a new occupation. I was a mental patient. My business was illness.

A fundamental principal of Dialectical Behavior Therapy is that every hospitalization represents a failure of therapy. My therapist tried to show me this. "Do you see what you're doing, Paul?" he would ask. "Every time life gets a little rough, you go to your doctor and say, 'I'm going to kill myself.' He does what he has to do. He puts you in the hospital. Don't you see that you are asking to be hospitalized, that you are manipulating your doctor into sending you there?" I was always indignant. I really did want to kill myself, for one thing. And I hated hospitals, for another. Why would I deliberately put myself in the position of going to one?

But the truth is, I had begun to work as hard at being mentally ill as I had at everything else. Since it had become my career, I applied to it all my old habits. And why did I want a career in mental illness? Because it was the path of least resistance. If I was ill, if I could assure myself that my problem lay in my brain chemistry, then nothing that had gone wrong in my life was my fault. I was absolved from personal responsibility for my actions. My failures could be attributed to my misfiring neurotransmitters rather than to anything I had done or not done. I had found a new, easy way to be successful. I could be sick without even trying. To be sure, this new career had its vexations. I had to endure hospitals. I had to submit to the ministrations of various professionals. I had to live cheaply. I had to agree to be useless. But there were two important respects in which I was freed. I didn't have to change. And I didn't have to expect anything of myself. Furthermore, this was socially acceptable. I was, after all, gravely ill.

An Exchange

Paul,

With all due respect, if you haven't read the books how can you make the summary judgment that you agree with your critic's assessment?

I don't understand your need to lacerate the previous work. I understand the feelings of disappointment and the desire to criticize and go beyond it—to write more candidly and to write something compelling.

But the work is a gift: It was given to you and you passed it on to us who appreciate it, who learned so much from it, who need it. And others you've not met who long for literature such as you have made.

So there you are, stuck between disappointment and the unborn who will inherit the work.

Lou

Lou,

You raise excellent questions.

The simple answer is that I was trying to explain how I got myself into my present situation. My attitude toward my books was an important factor in that process. But that, of course, is not an adequate answer.

A more complicated answer is that I have regarded my writing as an extension of myself. It has become, therefore, an extension of my self-hatred. I recognize intellectually that there are two delusions here. One is the delusion that my writing is me. The other is that my self-hatred is justified. These are deeply ingrained emotional habits. The first is at least twenty years old, the second at least fifty years old. I believe the fact that I'm writing again is a sign that I am beginning to change those habits. But I have a long way to go.

I understand depression, in this respect, as a defensive measure. In depression, your sense of yourself disappears. Hence the feeling of emptiness that people in severe depression often describe. When the self goes into hiding, it becomes less vulnerable to attack.

A healthy self, as you suggest, views both the life and its work as gifts. One may, as with any other kind of gift, be disappointed in what has been given and yet be grateful for it, knowing that the substance of the transaction lies not in the gift itself but in the act of giving.

To appreciate the giver more than the gift is, I would suppose, the essence of spirituality. It lies, at any rate, at the heart of the religion in which I was raised. You are a sinner, God says, but I love you all the same. You remind me that my favorite Bible verse as a child was, "God so loved the world that he gave His only begotten Son, that whosoever believeth in Him might be saved." I repeated that verse as a mantra during the day and said it as a prayer every night. I see now that it was the best effort I ever made at self-repair.

Paul

Change 3

I marched into my therapist's office the week after I quit my personality retraining with a bone to pick. "The problem with that stuff," I said, "is that it's trivial."

"Oh? And why is that?"

"You want to kill yourself, and they tell you to take a bubble bath or burn some incense."

"Well, when you put it that way, it does sound trivial," my therapist said. But, he reminded me, the Distraction Skills, as they are called in Dialectical Behavioral Therapy (DBT), are really much more complicated than that, and they are not meant as any kind of panacea. They are techniques to buy you a little time when you are impulsively bent on an irrational action.

I had to agree. But, I said, DBT is trivial in much more fundamental ways that that.

"Yes? Do you want to explain?"

"Well, for one thing, there is a big elephant sitting in the middle of the therapy room table. Every person there cuts himself, or abuses drugs, or thinks about suicide. But one of the ground rules is that we may not talk about these impulses. I understand why you wouldn't want the group to descend into one long pity party. But if you can't talk about the biggest obstacles in your life, you're not likely to talk about anything else that matters either."

"What do you mean?"

"Well, take last week. Anthony is there. He's just back from a trip to California to see about regaining custody of his kids. His kids have been with their foster parents since they were little. It's the only home they've known, the foster parents are the only real parents they've had, and California is the only place they've been. Anthony is wildly unstable. Every week, even though he's not supposed to, he talks about looking longingly at his bottles of pills and imagining downing them all at once. He's in a shaky second marriage that's just six months old. Neither he nor his wife is employed. What sort of favor does he think he's doing his kids by pulling them up from their roots, hauling them to Duluth, Minnesota, and establishing them in his household? Do we talk about that? Do we say, "Look, Anthony, stop thinking about yourself for one minute, and start considering what's best for your kids?" No. We talk about how well he used his DBT skills to stay cool in the face of the foster mother's hostility."

"Or take Thomas. He's a bright, articulate, able-bodied, cultured man, and he's working part time as a stock boy in a discount store. Do we say, 'What's wrong with this picture, Thomas?' No. He thinks the biggest problem in his life is keeping his cat boxes clean. We congratulate him on the steps he took last week to be more diligent about this chore."

"Or Jonathan. He's trying to maintain a relationship with his teen-aged daughter by micromanaging her life long-distance. Do we talk about the futility of that effort? No. We commended him on how well he prepared last week for his telephone conference with her English teacher about why she's only getting a B in the class."

"Or Mark. Every week he tells us how deeply in love he is with his wife. Then he relates some incident in which she has verbally abused him. Do we talk about why he needs such a lousy relationship? No. We applaud an alternative approach, one in which he tried to negotiate an end to her bullying."

"I could go on. But my point is, I undoubtedly am equally blind to my own destructive behaviors. I don't see how I'm going to get any better if someone doesn't point out to me what those behaviors are."

"Yes, you do have a point."

"And the proof of my concern is that I've been going to that group for a year now. Every week we sit around and rehearse the same petty grievances. And neither I nor anybody else in the group, so far as I can see, has made the least bit of improvement. Why bother?"

"Well, yes, I suspect that Marsha Linehan (the developer of the therapy) is a bit more confrontational than we are here."

Months later, I read my therapist's notes on this session. "Paul has not been in Dialectical Behavior Therapy skills group since 2/11/03," he wrote. "He feels that this approach to therapy is trivial. For example, when feeling like committing suicide "you are told to take a bubble bath or light an incense candle."' That's it. That's the entire report on our exchange. At the least, had I been the therapist, I might have discerned in those remarks a plea for help. I might have been tempted to say, "Well, Paul, maybe we can figure out what those destructive behaviors of yours are." But the notes for the session simply say, "He seems to be doing a huge turnaround."

This is one of many occasions in my long journey through several kinds of therapy when I've wondered why I bothered to say anything at all.

Therapy 2

A friend, the wise psychotherapist Mary Pipher, once said to me, in a moment of impatience, "When are you going to see, Paul, that a walk in the woods is less costly and more beneficial than any amount of therapy?"

Therapy 3

Then Eliphaz the Termite said:

Pain does not spring from the dust

    Or sorrow sprout from the soil:

Man is the father of sorrow,

    As surely as sparks fly upwards.

If I were you, I would pray:

    I would put my case before God.

You are lucky God has scolded you;

So take his lesson to heart.

For he wounds, but then binds up;

    He injures, but then he heals.

THE BOOK OF JOB

Suggestion from a Friend

You wouldn't be so depressed

if you really believed in God.

JANE KENYON

FROM THE POEM "HAVING IT
OUT WITH MELANCHOLY"

Therapy 4

Once, in a therapy group, a box was passed around the table. We were to draw from it a slip with instructions for an action that would make us feel better. My slip told me to go out and buy a new shirt. I ordinarily buy clothes in thrift stores but on this occasion I dutifully went to a department store in the local mall and bought a handsome and expensive new shirt. As instructed, I wore it to therapy the next day, and everybody told me that I looked very nice. I still have the shirt, and still wear it from time to time, but neither then nor at any time since then has it made me the least bit happier.

This is a strategy for coping with sorrow that both conventional wisdom and many popular therapies, including DBT, teach. When all else fails, distract yourself. Bite the bullet. Take a bubble bath. Light some incense. Do a little dance. But no amount of distraction will dispel sorrow. The only antidote to sorrow is to embrace it, to beseech it, that it might reveal to you what it wishes you to know.

Confession

Ideally, the therapy session would be an exercise in confession. But what if the confessor is charging three dollars a minute, is bound by professional protocol not to reveal himself as a fellow human being, and regards everything you say as potential evidence not of ordinary human fallibility, but of an abnormal pathology? How then is the confessant, known to his confessor as a "consumer," to make an honest and unguarded confession, the only kind that might prove useful?

The most abject of all needs is to confide, to confess. It's the soul's need to externalize.

FERNANDO PESSOA

Delusions 1

The moment you set out to fix something, it breaks. The first step in fixing a human being is not to want to. Souls shatter when they are struck with too many good intentions. That's the trouble with bad therapists: they mean to fix you up, set you on the path to right-thinking, get you to see how much better off you'd be if you traded in your delusions for theirs. But the only delusions a person can bear to live with are his own.

Delusions 2

There is nothing more dangerous than the man who believes that because he is popular, he is successful. Politics is so rotten precisely because it feeds upon this delusion. One of the powerful forces behind war, for example, is that leaders who wage it always enhance their poll numbers. Hitler was a product of evil, but he was also a product of his popularity.

In behavioral medicine, one form of popularity is "accepted practice." We don't know enough about how the brain works to understand why the accepted practices of the moment work, or even, in many cases, whether they do work. For example, a number of literature reviews have come to the conclusion that placebos are nearly as effective as drugs in the Prozac family at treating depression. And a recent study by the World Health Organization found that people with schizophrenia in the poorest countries, which do not have antipsychotic medications, have a better prognosis than schizophrenics in developed nations, who are routinely prescribed such drugs. Yesterday's accepted practices in cases of mental illness are today's cruelties. Psychotropic medications are the accepted practice of the moment, but that does not guarantee that they will be seen tomorrow as either humane or effective.

Delusions 3

Although my books were of no importance, at least I was spared the delusory experience of having them greeted as something else.

Objectivity

In order to make a science of despair, it is necessary to objectify pain. But if pain were not subjective, it could not be felt, and if it could not be felt, it would not exist. But if it did not exist, how could it be objectified? Here is one way in which therapy sometimes works: When you present yourself as a case to be studied, as an object, you cease to feel the pain that has bedeviled you. This absence of feeling produces a bright glow of relief. But the euphoria doesn't last long because it has come at the sacrifice of some part of your humanity.

Anger

I have been angry about some of the things that happened to me on my journey through mental illness. But why should I be angry? I learned from them, did I not? And is not learning a high calling?

I wanted those who treated me to be blameless, free from error, infinitely wise, long-suffering beyond understanding. I expected them to do for me what I had not been able to do for myself. I wanted them not to be human.

But they proved to be human after all, and so they taught me how to be content with being human myself. There is no greater gift than this.

Questions

I recently purchased an inexpensive beard trimmer. Enclosed in the package was a twenty-six item questionnaire. Where did I purchase my trimmer? How much did I pay? Did I buy it for myself or for someone else? Why did I select this brand? Was I satisfied with my purchase? If not, what didn't I like about it? How could the product be improved? Would I recommend that someone else purchase the same item? If not, why not? And so on.

This questionnaire reminded me that in the more than fifteen years that I have been a part of the mental health system, I have never once been asked, either informally or formally, by any provider institution or any individual provider how I felt about the care I had received.

I would hazard the wild assertion that mental health services are more important than beard trimmers. Why, then, do manufacturers of beard trimmers seem so much more concerned about what their customers think than do providers of mental health services? Is there nothing mental health providers might learn from their clients?

Reality 1

I know a man who, when he is not medicated, is constantly besieged by loud voices urging him to do violence against others. He has an acute case of paranoid schizophrenia. On medication, however, he is a rather passive and quite amiable man. Although he has few social skills, he is sufficiently recovered from his illness so that he has recently been able to work on a cleaning crew for a few hours a week, with the help of a job coach.

Outside of work, his life is totally absorbed in the consumption of movies featuring gratuitous violence or very low comedy and of heavy metal music. With respect to both of these interests, he displays a prodigious memory. Give him the first measure of almost any heavy metal song getting radio play in Duluth, Minnesota, and he can name the piece, identify the band, list its personnel, and recite the lyrics. I am astonished by this because although I have been a lifelong lover of music, every piece of heavy metal sounds exactly alike to me, one indistinguishable explosion of pure cacophony after another, the lyrics as unintelligible to me as if they were being sung in ancient Sumerian.

Likewise with movies. I believe it is not an exaggeration to say that this man can give a detailed, scene by scene account, including verbatim reports of key dialog and lyrics to the incidental music, for a hundred recent movies of the kind that film critics do not watch. His face becomes radiant when he is delivering these movie reviews. I find the recitations almost unbearably tedious, but since they are his only conversational gambit, I submit. And it has to be said, in fairness to him, that his plot summaries are at least on a par with those of public radio opera announcers.

He had a particular attraction to any song lyric or movie scene featuring the use of the word "fuck." In this, of course he may merely be reflecting his age. I live in a neighborhood of college students, and on the weekends, when the beer is flowing, the word "fuck" floats through my window dozens of times a day. And my friend enjoys repeating salacious jokes, for which he also has a prodigious memory.

As for his other qualities, the most notable is his occasional and, given his illness, quite astonishing capacity for empathy. I was feeling dizzy the other day. He suddenly took my hand to steady me as we passed down a city street, completely innocent of any consideration for what another pedestrian might make of two men walking hand-in-hand, one balding, the other much younger-looking than his late adolescence. I clutched his hand all the more tightly in appreciation of that innocence. I very much like being with him.

But he is totally, absolutely disinterested in reality of any kind. I told him the other day about a particular spectacular car crash I had witnessed on my street. It involved two demolished vehicles, two damaged houses, and two bloodied but living passengers. I thought it was something that might appeal to him, given his preoccupation with violent movies. And indeed that crash would have appealed to him had it taken place on a theater screen. But this was real life, and he couldn't have been more bored.

What does one say about a man who is, so far as I can tell, completely at peace with himself but who is just as completely disinterested in reality? Have his medications, in any meaningful sense, cured him of his mental affliction?

Of course, one could make much the same description of George II, chief executive of the most powerful nation on earth, who was thought by many (but not by me) to be not only sane but a hero.

Reality 2

I lived when I was very young in a three-room house, so the family slept together in one room. My parents occupied one bed and my twin sister and I were in the other. One summer, a tall, lanky man in a cowboy hat frequently invaded our bedroom just as we were about to drift off to sleep. He came in through the window, crept on tiptoes toward the bed my sister and I were in, and reached out to grab one or the other of us. Both of us saw him. Our descriptions of him matched. At the last moment before he managed to snatch one of us up, we screamed. When we did, he hastened out the window and fled in the dark. Even after he was gone, we continued to scream.

My father would get up with the flashlight. At first he was sympathetic, but he soon became annoyed. He would get us up and throw back the covers. He would shine the light on the window, which was always closed. He let us look under the bed. He took us through the other rooms in the house. "See, there is nobody here," he said. "No one. No man. No way for a man to get in. You were dreaming."

But he was there, we insisted. Both of us saw him.

"You *thought* you saw him. But we've looked everywhere he might be, and he isn't here. You've seen for yourself. Now go back to bed and let's try to get some rest."

He would tuck us in again, and we would fall asleep. But a day or two later, the man in the cowboy hat would be back again. He tormented us for a month or two. Finally he went away for good.

Although this happened at least fifty years ago, I can still see that man, as vividly as I did when I was a child. So can my sister. I know in my intellect, of course, that he could not have existed. But a part of me still believes in him. The same logic that was compelling to me as a child holds for me as a man. One of us might have been making this up. But *two* of us? And the image of him is so concrete and enduring.

I don't see bogeymen anymore, but I am still tormented by many convictions that are no more real. I have believed for many years that I am on the verge of bankruptcy, although I need only look at my bank balance to know that I still have plenty of money. I believe that all of my work has been utterly in vain, although there is sufficient objective evidence that that is not the case. I believe that people hate me who don't. I believe that people are trying to destroy me who aren't. It does no more good to tell me that these things aren't true than it did my father to lead us children around the house with a flashlight.

Once a good friend wrote to me in exasperation. "When you tell me something," she said, "I never know how much of it to believe." I have the same difficulty. I myself don't know what to believe.

The unfortunate truth is that what we believe is far more powerful than what we know. Our beliefs take on a reality that supersedes fact. This is as true for whole populations as it is for individuals. Two years after 9-11, seventy percent of Americans, including the Vice President, believed that Saddam Hussein had something to do with the attack. There is no evidence, as a matter of fact, that this is true. Everybody is, to some extent, deluded. We could not live in a world where we were always conscious of the plain truth and nothing but, especially about ourselves. Several studies suggest that one key difference between people who are optimists and people who are pessimists is that optimists consistently over-rate their own abilities. Within limits, to overestimate yourself is not a bad thing. Pessimists tend to be quite accurate about their abilities. That is not such a bad thing either.

I am a person who underestimates. I underestimate myself, my work, my effect on other people. With regularity there comes a point where I do so to the extent that I can't get out of bed, can't bear to see another human being, can't take pleasure in anything. That is the point at which the delusional becomes pathological.

The Delicate Balance

The art of living lies in the delicate balance between being honest enough about yourself to function in the world and not so honest as to self-destruct.

I don't know the meaning of this journey I was forced to make,
between one and another night, in the company of the whole universe.

FERNANDO PESSOA

Purpose

A life without purpose, like a watermelon without seeds.

Life Worth Living 1

The last hope of the person who is desperately depressed is that every life is worth living. When that hope fades, suicide becomes not only permissible but inevitable. A therapist says to a patient, "Let's talk about how you might build a life worth living." There is nothing compassionate or therapeutic in this remark. The corollary judgment upon which it depends is, "Your present life is not worth living." Or, more directly, "Your life, at least at this moment, is worthless." And that judgment depends upon three assumptions:

1) That life, as a thing in itself, is not valuable; you have got to do something (and I, your therapist, know what it is) in order to justify your existence.

2) That what you are doing now—suffering—is not useful, and

3) That suffering has no usefulness because it has no meaning.

During the eugenics movement of the first half of the twentieth century, this line of reasoning was carried to its logical conclusion. Harvard University's Earnest Hooten, in a book entitled *Apes, Men, and Morons*, described the insane as "specimens of humanity who really ought to be exterminated." The Nobel-Prize-winning physician Alexis Carrel wrote, in 1935, "Gigantic sums are now required to maintain prisons and insane asylums and protect the public against gangsters and lunatics. Why do we preserve these useless and harmful human beings? The abnormal prevent the development of the normal. This fact must be squarely faced. Why should society not dispose of the criminals and the insane in a more economical manner?" In 1940 and 1941, the Nazis, who took the eugenics movement to heart, executed 70,000 mental patients before dismantling the gas chambers and moving them east for the extermination of Jews, homosexuals, and other useless beings.

A therapist can challenge a patient to examine the ways in which his or her actions or beliefs sabotage the goals the patient is trying to achieve. A therapist can help a patient to find meaning in that suffering. A therapist can guide a patient to deeper thought about his or her purposes in life. A therapist can help a patient to appreciate the possibility that some aims are unachievable and that this does not matter. A therapist can help a patient to accept those things that are not changeable. But when the therapist proposes making a patient's life worth living or judges that the patient's present life is not worth living, he has, however unwittingly, crossed the line from therapy to contempt.

Life Worth Living 2

I know a man who was sent away to a mental hospital when he was thirteen. He spent his next thirty years in such places, during the darkest hours of psychiatric hospitalization. When his mother was aged and ill, he helped to support her by stealing the hospital's petty cash. He was never caught. When he was finally released, during the mass evacuations of mental hospitals in the 1970s, he moved to a tiny room in a squalid boarding home, where he still lives. He ekes out a meager existence by collecting aluminum cans, which he sells to a recycling center. You never see him without his plastic collecting bag. The possessions that he has accumulated during his lifetime would fit into a couple of fair-sized cardboard boxes. He is not a sociable man; he has, so far as I know, no friends. He does, however, have a passion for classical music. He listens to it with an intensity I have never before seen. He raises his eyes toward the ceiling, cocks an ear in the direction of the radio, and helps the conductor along with his hands. His eyes sparkle with an electric intensity, and his mouth is fixed in a beatific smile. When he listens to classical music, he radiates the beauty of his joy.

Has this man lived a life worth living? Not by any conventional account. But the generosity of his joy in music and the pluck with which he has scoured the streets of Duluth, Minnesota, for discarded cans have been to me wondrous gifts. I don't know how I could have lived without them, or him.

Practicalities 1

If you can't bring down the house, you might at least topple the porch.

Practicalities 2

I had been living in the darkness of the devil for days, too heavy with depression to rise from my bed. One day, a friend offered to visit me, and I locked the door against him and refused to answer the doorbell. I couldn't imagine summoning the energy to sit upright in his presence.

That night, I finally felt an emotion other than despair. I was incoherently angry at my brain, at its intransigent refusal, or so it seemed, to help me out a little. In my rage, I began to beat upon my head with my fists, shouting curses at my brain as I did so. Once I was started, I could not stop. I went at my head with all the might I could muster, over and over again. Bam! Bam! Bam! Bam! Bam! Bam! Bright, attractive images of my skull being shattered by a hammer floated through my consciousness. I gritted my teeth with each new blow. When I was at last sated, I fell asleep.

In the morning, my skull felt like a chocolate pudding, and every slight breeze wafting through the window hurt. But I spent the day on my feet, and laughed and laughed and kindled again the tiny, warm flame of hope.

Advice

Here's a kind of talk commonly heard among the mentally ill: "I didn't mean to yell at you the other day. That was just my illness talking." Or, "I'm sorry I missed your wedding. I was just too depressed." Or, "You'll have to excuse me when I interrupt you every time you try to speak. I'm a little manic right now." I know this kind of talk well because I frequently indulge in it myself.

And here's my advice: Every time you hear me saying something like this, politely, but very firmly, tell me to stuff it. Say, "If you're well enough to know you shouldn't have yelled at me, then you're also well enough to control your temper." Or, "I missed you at my wedding, too. You didn't skip it, however, because you were too depressed. You weren't there because you decided not to come." Or, "You know you shouldn't interrupt me. So stop doing it."

When I am ill, I am far too self-indulgent for my own good. You help to heal me when you demand that I, even though I am ill, practice the ordinary civilities.

Working the System 1

To be so mentally ill as to be disabled is to be at the bottom of the social heap. Your friends don't know quite what to do with you. You don't know what to do with yourself. People who know nothing else about you are afraid of you. Potential employers won't touch you. There is a social safety net of sorts, but public charity being what it is in the United States, that net supports you only at the level of abject poverty. The person you see downtown collecting the tobacco remnants out of used cigarette butts is probably mentally ill. Many of the people milling around outside the shelters for the homeless are mentally ill. So are many of the people standing in line at the soup kitchen. Chances are, if you are mentally ill, the only people you know who are actually making a living are the people treating you.

You may well be obese. Many psychotropic medications cause weight gain, and many cause sedation, and you can't afford a healthy diet on $550 a month, which is what people on Social Security Insurance currently get. Even with food stamps and a federal housing subsidy that limits your rent to a third of your income (if you can get one; in many places, the waiting list is years long, and you don't qualify if you have a criminal record, which a significant number of people who are mentally ill do) the money will not stretch to fresh fruit and vegetables. You are probably unkempt; it is expensive to maintain a decent wardrobe and keep it clean. You may stink, because of the bacteria breeding in the folds of your fat, or because the shower down the hall was busy when you wanted to use it or it didn't work again, or because you have been too ill recently to care about hygiene. You are, in short, scum.

The miracle is that so many people who are mentally ill manage as well as they do. I'd like to see how the President or any of the leaders of the Congress would fare if put for three months, say, on a strict budget of $550 a month, no cars, no telephones, no aides, no dinner parties with friends, no credit cards or bank accounts to fall back on, but weekly visits to a social worker to be included. I'd like to see a social worker asking Dennis Hastert or Tom Daschle, "And when was the last time you bathed? Have you been brushing your teeth? Do you have lice?" I'd like them to be on medications that made them sleepy, lethargic, and impotent. I'd like one of them to be on a drug that made him wet the bed. I'd like Bill Gates and Warren Buffett to try it out for a year. I would like to know whether they felt as confident about themselves at the end of the year as they had at the beginning.

When I became disabled by mental illness, I had supported myself for forty years. The most difficult thing about accepting disability was giving up my independence which, it turned out, had a lot to do with how I regarded myself. It wasn't just the money, although I hate being on the public dole. More degrading, in a way, was the platoon of caring sorts who were assigned to look after various aspects of me. At one point, I was under the supervision of a psychiatrist, a psychiatric nurse practitioner, an individual therapist, a group therapist, an outreach nurse, a case manager, and a legal guardian. All of them felt, quite properly, that it was their business to know how I was feeling, what I was thinking, and what I was doing. This was not to say that I disliked any of those people. On the contrary, I thought most of them were terrific, and I appreciated the many things they did for me. But there were times when I felt like a child with seven babysitters.

And these were not the only caretakers I had to worry about. On one occasion I left an institution and walked home on a bitterly cold January night. The police were summoned to my doorstep. (How many of us, I once asked a group of ten people who were mentally ill, have been handcuffed? Eight of us raised our hands.) On at least two other occasions (there are significant gaps in my memory so there may have been more), members of the local Crisis Response Team, alerted by one of my caretakers, came to my house and took me away to be institutionalized. Twenty minutes to get the gentle ultimatum and five minutes to pack. I had become, in a way, an item of public property shuffled from one temporary storage facility to another.

But I am aware that I have been spared worse indignities. I know, for example, a middle-aged woman, the mother of two adult children, who lives, by order of the court, with foster parents, who hire a sitter for her when they have to go out. She frequently talks with indignation about the time, quite recently, when she was made, in a hospital psychiatric ward, to sleep in a crib, a "baby crib," she always insists. Perhaps there were safety reasons for keeping her there, but that does not, in the least, alleviate the woman's embarrassment. It would defy the best of us to maintain a healthy sense of dignity while being treated exactly like an infant.

I remember a night on a psychiatric ward when a nurse woke an incontinent patient to change his diaper. "Well, hello there," she said, in a voice loud enough to wake me five or six doors down the hall but in the tone of a mother cooing to her baby, "I think we had better change those pants. It's time to get some nice dry pants. Something not so wet and yucky." And then, "There, now we've got nice new pants, haven't we? All clean and dry again." That man was sleeping in a crib, too. He had been given not a patient version of it, but a toddler's sippy-cup, complete with nursery decals, to drink from. It is the policy on the same ward to keep patients who are bed-bound and incontinent in just pajama tops and diapers, dispensing with the bottoms that might offer them some bit of privacy. I once inquired about the reason for this policy. I got, of course, no answer. The patient's role is not to question, but to submit.

But there always are, even in the most difficult situations, ways of coping. One technique that I have admired, although I have not been able to imitate it, is to talk about the people tending you in the same way that the President talks about his undersecretaries, or that a business tycoon talks about his minions. "I said to my worker today, if you don't come through with that bus pass by Thursday, I'm going to fire you." Or, "My worker said I should go to day treatment, and I told her, 'You'd better come up with another idea before I fire your ass.'" Or, "I told my worker he'd better get on my payee's case or my psychiatrist is going to know the reason why." The imperial fashioned out of the demeaning. Like a movie director on Oscar night: "But I could not have done it without my wonderful staff."

And in truth, "workers" can be fired, or at least gotten rid of. It's something that no doubt drives social workers up the wall, but I'm all for it.

Class

There is one way in which my descent into disability through mental illness felt like a welcome homecoming. I was born and raised on a small subsistence farm. Even in the little rural high school that I attended, I was very much a kid from the wrong side of the tracks. When it came time for me to go to college, I chose to study, at my own expense, at a public university rather than at one of the private colleges that had offered me generous scholarships. I did not think I could make the social leap that would be required of me, nor did I relish the idea of being the token hick. In time, through very little effort of my own, I became modestly wealthy. I had, at any rate, a good deal more money than any one person is entitled to. Not long after I acquired it, I had a nervous breakdown. The deep anxiety I felt over being in possession of so much money, and the feeling that I was a traitor to my class, were certainly significant factors in that breakdown. I knew for a fact that the money had come at the expense of many people much more deserving than I, dear friends of mine, with whom I had lost all contact because I was too ashamed of what had transpired to face them. In my heart, I knew then, I could never be anything but a member of the lowest class. By and by, through the agency of mental illness, I arrived at that status again in fact as well as spirit. In that respect, at least, I believe that I had been blessed. I am reaffirmed in what I take to be a fundamental truth: anyone who pursues profit for the sake of profit does evil.

Working the System 2

I know a woman who is frequently arrested for public drunkenness but seldom spends much time in detox, where the staff tends to treat you as if you have SARS. "As soon as I get to detox," she says, "I say that I am going to kill myself. Right away, the staff calls an ambulance and has me sent to a psychiatric ward. I spend the night there. In the morning, I'm sober again, and I say, 'What? Kill myself? That was just the booze talking.' What are they going to do? Psych wards don't like drunks anyway. By mid-morning, I'm on the streets again."

Paradoxes

The richest life is one in service to others. But the freedom to pursue such a life requires a steady sense of self. You must believe that you have something to offer to others before you can offer it. But what if your sense of yourself is fractured? What then? The paradox is that healing may depend upon learning to act as if the fracture didn't exist. But every available psychotherapy intensifies the preoccupation with self. Could it be that existing psychotherapies aggravate the wounds, delaying the moment when one can walk out of the self and into the wide and satisfying world?

Here's another paradox. People who are mentally ill are often remarkably empathetic. Pain seems to search out pain as water seeks the level. But this empathy goes nowhere because it only multiplies one's awareness of one's own pain. It often becomes, in people who are mentally ill, a virtue without reward. The only remedy that I know of lies in peer-led support groups, which teach the art of directing empathy in a positive way towards others. They lead the mentally ill into lives of service. The remarkable success of AA groups is a notable example of this idea in action.

Why are peer-led groups so little used in psychotherapy? The simplest answer is the likeliest. They operate outside the money economy. Mental health professionals can't charge for them.

I don't think we'll have a truly successful mental health system until the mentally ill become genuine partners in their own healing, and the only way to do that is to make them healers, rather than merely the objects of healing.

Semantics 1

We say that one *gets* cancer, or a cold, or kidney disease. One would never think to say that one *is* cancer. But we say that one *is* depressed, or bipolar, or schizophrenic. A disease of the body is a condition. But a disease of the mind, we think, is a state of being. We no longer believe, as we did 250 years ago, that the mentally ill are animals, but we are not yet ready to grant that they are fully human either.

Semantics 2

In the parlance of medicine, drugs have effects, and then they have side-effects. There is something reassuring in this language. Side-effects are to effects, the suggestion is, as cranberry sauce is to roast turkey. This reassurance vanishes, however, when one realizes that the "side-effects" of some drugs are fatal. In such cases, the proper analogy is, side effects are to effects as strychnine is to roast turkey.

One of the drugs I take is Effexor. Its "effects" are to relieve depression and generalized anxiety. These are its "side-effects": abnormal dreams, abnormal ejaculation or orgasm, anxiety, appetite loss, blurred vision, chills, constipation, diarrhea, dizziness, dry mouth, frequent urination, flushing, gas, headache, impotence, infection, insomnia, muscle tension, nausea, nervousness, rash, sleepiness, sweating, tingling feeling, tremor, upset stomach, vomiting, weakness, yawning, abnormal taste, abnormal thinking, agitation, chest pain, confusion, decreased sex drive, depression, dilated pupils, dizziness upon standing up, high blood pressure, fluid retention, itching, loss of identity, rapid heartbeat, ringing in the ears, trauma, twitching, urinary problems, and weight loss. It is worth noting that Effexor can cause the same conditions it is intended to relieve, namely depression and anxiety.

It is true, of course, that no one person will experience all of these "side" effects, that some of them are quite rare, and that some people will experience none of them. But they are all possible, and in some cases, their cumulative effects may be as bad or as worse than the "cure."

Every drug has many effects. Some of them are desirable and some are not. If one were to avoid euphemisms, therefore, one would speak not of effects and side-effects, but of beneficial effects and adverse ones.

Semantics 3

At one time, my primary diagnosis was bipolar disorder. Until the end of the Nineteenth Century, people with bipolar disorder were called lunatics. Hence the term "lunatic asylum." This name was based on the belief that our variable moods were influenced by the phases of the moon. Some other names we have been called: abnormal, absurd, alien, around the bend, ass, balmy, batty, bedlamite, bereft of reason, bonkers, borderline case, brainsick, buffoon, clown, cockeyed, crackbrained, cracked, crackers, crackpot, crank, crazed, crazy, daft, deluded, dement, demented, demoniac, deprived of reason, deranged, ding-a-ling, dippy, distraught, doodle, dopey, dotty, egregious ass, fanatic, fantastic, figure of fun, flake, flighty, gaga, hallucinated, harebrained, idiot, ignoramus, imbecilic, insane, irrational, jackass, jerky, kook, loco, loon, loony, loopy, mad, mad as a hatter, maddened, madman, mental, mentally deficient, meshuggah, messed up, milksop, mooncalf, moonstruck, moronic, neuropath, neurotic, non compos, non compos mentis, nonsensical, not all there, not right, nut, nutty as a fruitcake, odd, of unsound mind, off, paranoid, out of one's head, preposterous, perfect fool, phrenetic, potty, psycho, psychoneurotic, queer, raver, raving lunatic, reasonless, sappy, silly, schmuck, screwball, screwy, senseless, sick in the head, softhead, sop, stark-mad, stark raving mad, strange, stupid ass, tetched, tomfool, touched, unearthly, unhinged, unsane, unsettled, unsound, wacky, wandering, weirdo, witless, zany.

It is interesting to note how many of these names, their connections to the mentally ill long forgotten, remain in widespread use as terms of scorn.

Credentials

The person who wears a PhD like a cloth coat generally has nothing else to wear.

Insanity in individuals is something rare—but in groups, parties, nations, and epochs—it is the rule.

FRIEDRICH NIETZSCHE

Preening 1

I have in front of me the announcement of a conference for practicing psychiatric nurses. The conference is called, "Managing Clinical Practice Through Science." This would seem a dauntingly broad subject, but the conference turns out not actually to be about "science" in any general sense; it is about psychopharmacology, the use of drugs to treat mental illness. That is, for all practical purposes, what psychiatry has come to be. It is not a surprise to see that the "grantors" of this event are several pharmaceutical companies.

One of the sessions has the title, "Getting to the Heart of the Brain: Can We Finally Get It that Addiction is a Brain-Based Disease?" This session, the announcement brochure tells us, "will describe the extant research on genetic and environmental etiological factors that are neuroprotective and those known to promote disease vulnerability. The new brain-based model will be contrasted to the traditional model of substance abuse and the clinical implications of the brain-based model will be used as the rationale for new, brain-based pharmacological interventions that support the identified brain deficits." It is possible, with some difficulty, to translate this into English: the session will discuss research about genetic and social factors influencing addictions. If we see addicts as brain-diseased rather than as drug abusers, the session's organizer promises, then we will have the rationale we need to treat drug dependency with drugs rather than therapy.

This is as pure an exhibition of the idea of "better living through chemistry" as I've seen. One striking thing about it is the way in which it sweeps the social factors involved in addiction under the rug. If addiction to one drug really can be cured by prescribed dependency upon another, then communities can be absolved of responsibility for correcting those social maladies that foster addiction. At the same time, addicts are relieved of any individual responsibility for the conduct or consequences of their lives: it was not me, it was my brain deficits; I don't need to change a thing about my life or my outlook on it, I just need to switch drugs. Stating the problem of addiction in this way undermines social and individual responsibility, the very pillars upon which healthy communities are built. It makes mental health into a private transaction between an individual and his psychiatrist, one in which the psychiatrist, acting entirely alone, effects the cure, leaving both the individual and the community without any interest or standing in matter of public health or the common good.

Preening 2

I took, at the University of Minnesota, a seminar called "The Meaning of Life." It was taught by the brilliant poet and teacher John Berryman, the only professor on campus, even then, who could have gotten by with such a title. The seminar turned out to be an exploration of various literary portraits of love, from the erotic poems of Sappho to the ecstatic love of Teresa of Avila, from the tragedy of *Madame Bovary* to the comedy of *The Tempest*, from Norman O. Brown's psychoanalytic pairing of love and money to Anne Frank's heroic love of humanity. It really was a seminar about life and its meaning, not in the abstract, but in the particular, and in the here and now. We wept in that classroom, and we exploded with intellectual excitement, and together we experienced moments of great joy. I have never forgotten it.

Were the same class to be offered today by some English department, it would be entitled, "It Takes Two to Tango: Praxis, Politics, and (Dis)ingenuities in the Discourse of Lov(ers) for the Postmodern Era," (the title of a paper the professor had read to great acclaim at Barnard). The text would be twenty-seven inscrutable exercises in literary theory (the references cited in the professor's Barnard paper) and three poems by Nikki Giovanni. Ten minutes after it had ended, not one student would be able to remember a single thing about it.

Professionals 1

I tried to schedule my therapy appointments first thing in the morning, believing that if I had to get up anyway, there was a fighting chance that I might stay on my feet for the better part of the day. Before I went in, I made it a habit to stand at the back entrance to the clinic and have a last cigarette. The television set in the waiting room of the clinic, which catered mostly to adults, was always on. It was always turned to a child's channel. Those perky kids and their hyperactive hosts drove me bananas. I hated yet another reminder that I was really just a child. So I smoked.

I didn't need to look at my watch to know when it was time to go in. Every morning at precisely the last minute, one of the therapists drove the wrong way up the one-way alley, parked in the same no-parking spot, blocking access by the handicapped to the building across the way, and climbed, with a scowl on her face, out of her massive SUV. She strode across the alley wearing the sort of boots favored by dominatrixes, brushed past me without apology or a good morning, and went in.

In my more masochistic moments, I have fantasized being a patient of hers.

Professionals 2

I was living in a former one-car garage that had been converted into a tiny apartment, the only thing I could afford. The place was dark and cramped, and exceedingly quiet. There was me, there was the dull sound of the flame in the fuel oil burner, and sometimes there was the sound of the wind wailing against the walls. I was extremely depressed. I started thinking that I would do better if I were around people more. I became so desperate that I considered moving into a group home, a place that did "foster care," even though that would have been another downward step in my spectacular plunge from competency into official madness. My case manager, a man at least twenty-five years my junior, and I went to look at the place. The program director met us at the door. He might have been able to buy a beer legally, but you couldn't have told that from looking at him. He shook hands with us and invited us in. From that moment on, I became a cipher.

"This is where he would stay," the program director said to my case manager. He had already forgotten my name. I looked into the room. It was half the size of the one in which I was staying, and there were two beds, one of them obviously already occupied.

"And this is the dining room. This is where he would eat. We also do crafts twice a week in this room. We like to try to keep our residents active, and they seem to enjoy the crafts. And this is the living room. This is where he could watch TV or just relax. There's another room with a TV on the lower level." I didn't have a television set in the place where I was staying, on purpose. "And the other bedrooms are down this hall," he said pointing.

The young man directed us to seats in the living room. "Do you have any questions?" he asked my case manager.

"Not right now," he said.

"Well, I have a couple of questions," the program director said. "Is he able to go out on his own, or will he need an escort?"

"No, he's quite independent."

"Does he dress himself?"

"Yes."

"Will he need help in the shower?"

"No."

"We, of course, will manage his medications for him."

"Yes."

"Any special dietary needs?"

"He has diabetes."

"Of course, several of our residents do. That would be no problem. Does he manage his own money?"

"Yes."

"Any other special needs?"

"No."

"Is there anything else I can help you with?"

"Not really, thank you."

"All right then. Let me know what you decide." The young man stood up, led us to the door, and shook hands with my case manager, but not with me. We walked out into the driveway. I looked dolefully at my case manager, and he looked at me. We were both shaking our heads.

After that I felt quite a bit better in my old garage for some time. There's nothing like a vision of hell to cheer a person up.

Professionals 3

I know a man, a playwright, who has struggled for years to achieve an audience and professional recognition, hardly unusual for an artist. He was in agony about the need to rely entirely upon his wife for support in order to continue what he believed to be his life's work. He went to a therapist, seeking advice about how to deal with this conflict. He told his story. She said that she knew what he was talking about since she herself was a fairly good poet for a therapist.

Then she asked, "Have you ever had a play produced on Broadway?"

No he hadn't, the man admitted. As he had just explained . . .

"You're no Byron, you know," she said. (Byron suffered from what is now called bipolar disorder.)

Then she ordered the man to parade around her Victorian house while she observed and took notes. "I felt like the Elephant Man," he said.

"You have a subtle stiffness," she pronounced, as who wouldn't have had? The man, as it happens, has been a life-long and quite good amateur athlete.

And then—she had not read a line of his work and knew next to nothing about his life—she announced her diagnosis: he was narcissistic and grandiose, and his work, in consequence, was inflated and born of the same pathologies. He had, moreover, an addictive personality. It was too bad he was not addicted to drugs or alcohol, she said, because AA would be the treatment of choice.

Then she dismissed him.

She promptly sent a bill for her services. A week later, she sent a second bill. The envelope bore a notice stamped in red: OVERDUE.

Sanity

The United States Supreme Court has decided to let stand a ruling allowing prison officials to forcibly medicate a man in order to make him sane enough to execute. Of course, medications won't make the man sane. There is no known medical cure for insanity. The drugs will merely alleviate the active symptoms of his illness. So the law of the land is that you may not execute a man who is insane unless prison officials drug him into appearing to be sane, in which case the killing may proceed. The state killing, in turn, is motivated by the fact that the man in question killed someone. It is illegal to kill someone. To do so is morally repugnant, unless the state does the killing, in which case it is justified by the need to discourage killing.

Sometimes it is hard, without a program, to tell what's sane and what isn't.

Things to Come

In the early part of the 21st century, Lake Lewisville, near Dallas, Texas, was polluted with fluoxetine, the active ingredient in Prozac. It is thought that the substance originated in the urine of users of Prozac pills flushed down toilets. The chemical was also found in the tissues of the lake's blue gills, although at sub-therapeutic levels.

The best revenge is not to be like that.

MARCUS AURELIAS

Recovery

The first sign of recovery from depression is the realization that other people suffer, too.

It was a great and cleansing shock to me to learn one day that my psychiatrist was not happy either.

Prayer

You have lent to me, Lord, this desk, these clothes, this cup of coffee, this house, this day, this life, this bountiful world, this vast universe. In exchange, you have asked only that I use them well. Help me to see that they are not mine.

This sadness, this screaming, this emptiness, this loss, they are also yours, Lord, and they are also gifts. Let me receive them with a grateful heart. Help me to use them well.

When the time comes, I pray that I might relinquish these gifts freely, for they were freely given. Help me to see that this is my gift.

Happiness 1

Psychologist John Brantner once said to a group of his peers, "The first thing we should be asking our clients is, 'Whoever gave you the idea that you *ought* to be happy all the time?'"

Don't let your imagination be crushed by life as a whole. Don't try to picture everything bad that could possibly happen. Stick with the situation at hand and ask, "Why is this so unbearable? Why can't I endure it?" You'll be embarrassed to answer.

Then remind yourself that past and future have no power over you. Only the present—and even that can be minimized. Just mark off its limits. And if your mind claims it can't hold out against that . . . well, then, heap some shame upon it.

MARCUS AURELIUS

The gods are gods

Because they don't think

About what they are.

FERNANDO PESSOA

Happiness 2

Yesterday, I picked up a young man who cannot drive because of his seizures, and we went to Minneapolis to visit a young woman, a mutual friend. She was born with fetal alcohol syndrome. Her mother fed her booze in her baby bottle. She was an alcoholic by the time she was twelve. A new treatment for schizophrenia, one of the few drugs she hadn't tried, had just failed. But we resolved to forget about all that. We took in the lively downtown scene, shopped for things we couldn't buy, the more outrageous, the better; planned the young woman's imaginary campaign for governor; lingered over a good meal; and laughed a great deal. When we returned her to the hospital we were all in a fine mood.

A dozen years ago, before I was brought to my knees by mental illness, I could not have afforded such a day. I was much too busy being impressive. But along the way, I learned something more important than making an impression; I finally began to see what it might take to be happy.

Happiness 3

A man I know was just starting in business when he was twenty-three. He had recently bought a new car that he was very proud of. He was also proud of his accomplishments as an amateur athlete. Then one day, in a fit of despair, he parked his car in the garage, attached a hose to the exhaust pipe and ran it though the back window, got in, and started the engine. He was discovered before he was dead, but not before he had done grave damage to his brain.

He had to start all over again. He had to learn how to walk and talk, how to feed and dress himself. Some things were beyond him, however. He never learned to read again. He can walk, but not run. He can talk, but only people who know him well can understand him. He can sign his name, but not legibly. He can tie his shoes, but not well enough to keep them tied. He likes to fish, but he can't bait the hook or throw out the line. He wishes he could ride a bike, roller skate, get a job, live alone, but all of these things are now impossible. He has become a child of five or six in a man's body, with one exception: he can remember who he was and what he could do before his accident, as he calls it.

Here is a snapshot of him on a recent trip to Disney World. He is standing with a companion in front of a Goofy mascot. His grin is, if anything, wider than the mascot's. There is a dark stain on his shorts. He has wet his pants.

"One thing has changed since my accident," he said to me one day.

"Oh?" I said, "and, what is that?"

"Now, I am happy."

Happiness 4

The writer Bill Holm once said to me, in an estimate not far wide of the mark, "You know, Paul, I believe that I am one of six remaining extroverts in Minnesota." I remembered that remark as I was sitting in the lounge on the "open" psychiatric ward of a local hospital. From my seat, I had a clear view of the long corridor of the "locked" ward. (Both wards are securely locked. The difference is that the "open" ward has slightly better furniture.) Down it strode a very tall and very big man. He held his head high and he took his time. He moved as if he owned the place, as if he were the lord or prince of it. He marched steadily, unflinchingly forward until he had reached the windows of the nursing station. Two nurses piled out of the nursing station door, wrapped the man in a blanket, and hustled him back down the corridor to his room. He had been stark naked.

When he emerged again fifteen minutes later, he was dressed in regulation uniform of puke-green scrubs and tan hospital socks, and he had lost all of his magnificent bearing. He looked like any other slightly disoriented psychiatric ward denizen.

The next morning, I was at my station, and he made the same triumphal, nude march down the hospital corridor, was hustled once again into a blanket, and once more made his reappearance as an ordinary man clothed in scrubs. He did the same the morning after that, and the morning after that. And then I was discharged and felt bereft for several days without my morning spectacle.

I don't know what the nurses were so excited about. It was not as if they or we had never seen a naked man before. And the man was quite right about one thing, whatever his other confusions may have been. His nudity became him. He was not, it is true, a body anyone would think to sculpt. He had the kind of belly that takes on a personality all its own, and his chest was sunken and hairy, and his legs were bowed, and he had the penis of a boy. But he was perfectly happy in that body and delighted to share his pleasure with anybody who cared to look. I cared to look, and every morning for the duration of his brief march, I was happy with him.

If the unlikely day ever comes when I decide to cross over into the company of Minnesota's six extroverts, I plan to emulate him.

Happiness 5

One recent afternoon, I managed, after a struggle, to heave myself out of the bed in which I had been lying for four days. After another struggle, I overcame my inertia a second time and willed myself out the door. Three blocks from my apartment there was a path I had been meaning to explore for the last year. It is one of several dozen creeks in my town, Duluth, Minnesota, that fall out of the highlands until they reach slopes gentle enough to permit houses. Then the streams disappear into buried culverts only to emerge again on the shores of Lake Superior.

The path was wide and well-trodden, but I had not climbed a block before I felt that I was traversing a wilderness trail. The wind babbled in the canopies of the tall cottonwoods, and the water warbled across the stones. I climbed steadily, dully taking in the music of the canyon. It seemed both to calm me and to give me the energy I needed to keep going. Gradually, the canyon narrowed, bringing the path closer to the water. The cottonwoods gave way to pines.

About half way up, a group of boys played in the pool at the bottom of a waterfall. They played as boys played, with a great noise, taunting and daring each other, and clamoring for attention. They reminded me of the hours I spent as a boy dallying with my cousins at the edge of every bit of water that presented itself: the drainage ditch, the cattail marsh, the puddles after a rainfall. It was the first time in more than a week that I had a memory and the experience of it felt as bracing as a shot of Scotch. I couldn't remember the last time I had a feeling that was not leaden.

Higher still, I passed under a street bridge that was being repaired, and I remembered, with astonishment, that I was in a city. "All this, and a city, too!" I rejoiced. It seemed to me that it had been months since I had been moved to exclamation.

And then, rounding a curve in a very narrow passage of the canyon, I was met face-to-face with a burst of wind. I felt its delicious coolness on my cheeks. There was another sensation. It took me a moment to place it. Pines! It was the scent of pines! I could smell again! Looking up, I saw the majestic sweep of the white pines towering overhead, but it was the fact that I could smell them, not that they were there, that seemed to me so extraordinary, so marvelous.

And then it was as if the whole world had suddenly unfrozen. The heads of the pines tossed in the wind, and the mosses on the rocks gleamed green and red, and the rocks themselves seemed to arch and twist in a sprightly dance with the water. There were smells and noises, colors and textures in every direction.

And then I noticed—its arrival had escaped my attention—that it was beginning to be autumn. White and purple asters bloomed, jewelweeds sparkled, goldenrods turned every sunny nook brilliant yellow. The blue fruits of the bluebeard lilies vied with the scarlet hips of the wild roses for attention. I began to see again, and to strain—it had been so long—for the names of the understory plants, the mountain maples and ferns and thimbleberries, the birches and ashes, the club mosses and spikenards. I ran their names over my tongue as if they were draughts of cool water. I could feel the sweat on my body and taste it on my lips, and it was good. All of it was very good.

And then I had reached the top of the canyon, and, turning, I saw the houses of the city, and the lift bridge through which pass the freighters of both inland and the salty seas, and the great blue expanse of Lake Superior. I felt, for a sentimental moment, as if I might burst out, like Julie Andrews, in a chorus of "The Hills Are Alive with the Sound of Music."

I made my way down the canyon again, calling out the names of my friends, the Northwood's plants, as if I were a politician working a hometown parade. When I got back to my apartment, my left knee throbbed, but I was alive, indisputably alive. The feeling of vitality lingered for two days. The darkness, as it does, closed in again, but I had the conviction this time that, if I could just get there, I knew where to go to find the light.

Awaken: return to yourself. Now, no longer sleep, knowing they were only dreams; clear headed again, treat everything around you as a dream.

MARCUS AURELIUS

Sufficiency

I should like to have written something learned and wise, but I am no scholar and although I am growing old, I am not wise. The only thing I know is myself, and that not very well. Still, it might be sufficient. As Walt Whitman said, "A mouse is miracle enough to stagger sextillions of infidels."

Thank You

Thank you, dear reader. I have been restoring myself through the agency of these words. Your attentiveness has been most helpful. Please do not, however, though you have earned it, send me a bill.

About the Author

Paul Gruchow, once described as our contemporary Thoreau, wrote on subjects ranging from the culture of the tall grass prairie to what we teach (and fail to teach) rural children. His work is widely acclaimed for its lyrical prose and eloquence. A respected and inspiring educator, Paul Gruchow's writer in residence involvements included St. Olaf and Concordia Colleges, The University of Minnesota, The Lake Superior Studies Program, as well as lectures and workshops in public schools, churches, bookstores, government and environmental organizations. He won both the Minnesota Book and Lifetime Achievement Awards and in the 1980's edited *The Worthington Globe,* an award-winning newspaper. Paul Gruchow took his own life in Duluth, Minnesota, on February 22, 2004, at the age of 56.

Also by Paul Gruchow

Journal of a Prairie Year (University of Minnesota Press, 1985)

The Necessity of Empty Places (St. Martin's Press, 1988; reprinted, Milkweed Editions, 1999, 10th Anniversary Edition with a new preface by the author.)

Minnesota: Images of Home (Photography by Jim Brandenburg. Meriden-Stinehour Press, 1990)

Travels in Canoe Country (Little, Brown and Company, 1992)

Grass Roots: The Universe of Home (Milkweed Editions, 1995)

Boundary Waters: The Grace of the Wild (Milkweed Editions, 1997)

Worlds Within a World: Reflections on Visits to Minnesota Scientific and Natural Area Preserves (Minnesota, Department of Natural Resources, 1999)